discovering the

WARRIOR
IN YOU

DESTINY IMAGE® PUBLISHERS, INC.
P.O. Box 310, Shippensburg, PA 17257-0310

"Publishing cutting-edge prophetic resources to supernaturally empower the body of Christ"

This book and all other Destiny Image and Destiny Image Fiction books are available at Christian bookstores and distributors worldwide.

For more information on foreign distributors, call 717-532-3040.

Reach us on the Internet: www.destinyimage.com.

ISBN 13: 978-0-7684-7536-4

ISBN 13 eBook: 978-0-7684-7537-1

For Worldwide Distribution, Printed in the U.S.A.

1 2 3 4 5 6 7 8 / 27 26 25 24 23

discovering the
WARRIOR IN YOU

David: The Making of a King

PAUL E. TSIKA

DEDICATION

Warriors come in all sizes, shapes, colors, ethnic groups, and backgrounds. Some come from less than desirable beginnings and some from more privileged beginnings. Some are female and some are male; some are young and some are older.

But I believe they all have one thing in common—a brave heart.

Finding a person with a brave heart is one thing, but finding a warrior with a godly, brave heart is quite another.

Even as I write these lines, one face, one name, one person comes to mind above all the other brave hearts I know.

I met her in early 1966 and fell head over heels in love with her almost immediately. We married within two months. This year we will celebrate 58 years together as husband and wife.

I could and probably should write an entire book about this woman. She's been the greatest gift (besides Christ and the Holy Spirit) that God the Father has ever gifted me.

She is in every way a godly wife, mother of three with their spouses, grandmother to eleven, and great-grandmother to fifteen.

I find myself thanking God on an almost daily basis for her life.

As a believer she has been a rock for me, truly the backbone of this tribe, and the stabilizer of my thinking time and time again.

She has encouraged me when I needed encouragement, confronted me in love when I've needed correction, and has *always* been a faithful, godly wife. If you want to know more about her you can read her story in Proverbs 31:10-31.

I joyfully dedicate this book to my precious wife, Billie Kaye Rexroad Tsika, she is the greatest warrior I know. The greatest warrior I know.

Honey, I love you desperately.

ACKNOWLEDGMENTS

Destiny Image: Our partnership with this organization has been a blessing for our entire family and ministry. They have undertaken projects for us since 2010. Their staff has always been accommodating, responsible, and extremely helpful. Destiny's ministry is worldwide, and we're thankful and honored to be amongst their family of writers. A special 'thank you' to Christian Rafetto and Lisa Ott for being amazing with your input.

Gretchen Ann (Tsika) Rush: My precious, priceless daughter who serves our ministry in ways most never see. She's been a tremendous source of encouragement with her availability to proof our books over and over. Thanks, sweetheart. I love you.

Dr. J. Tod Zeiger (todzeigerministries.com): My fellow co-laborer in my ministry of writing. Tod has a pastor's heart and mind when it comes to loving God's people, communicating the Word of God, and writing. Tod has pastored churches, built colleges, he travels and speaks, and still finds time to help me with his gifts. Thank you, Tod, you're a blessing.

Thomas J. Tsika: My CFO and partner in our ministry. He oversees everything, including me. God has enlarged our tents of ministry and

Thom has always risen to the occasion. His wife has greatly contributed to the ministry with her "Lumi" children's books. And now his oldest daughter is making her debut with her first book coming out this year. Thanks, son, for all you do for Mom and me. I could not do what I do without you. I love you.

Paul E. Tsika II: I want to acknowledge my oldest son, Paul II, because he has exemplified a warrior's heart of compassion and mercy. His heart is strong but tender, and God is greatly using him to help strengthen me in my latter years. He's a faithful son, great friend, and fellow laborer for the cause of Christ. I love you, Paul, and I'm always here for you.

CONTENTS

PREFACE

T here are many characteristics of a warrior's heart and life. They have an unwritten creed that resonates within them constantly. It's not their talk, it's their walk that separates them from the rest of the pack. It's not really definable—it's an unspoken confidence, a presence, a spirit that is unmistakable. You just know when you're around them that they are different because they make you feel safe. They never try to intimidate you, but neither are they able to be intimidated. They're strong but not unkind; they're just but not unbending; righteous but not self-righteous.

For me, a brave-hearted warrior attempts to live a God-centered life and desires for the Word of God to be the determiner of their life and decisions.

They have purpose and live a life that exemplifies that purpose.

They have an unseen mission that becomes obvious when you're around them.

They have a sense of destiny that continues to unfold day by day.

They have a mission placed in their heart by God. When they're young, they can't see it in themselves as clearly as older visionaries can.

At the end of the day, they are the relentless ones, the focused ones, the passionate ones, and the ones who live a calculated life.

Something deep within their spirit burns out all the dross of fear, doubt, and cowardness.

They don't just live life, they attack life with a recognizable passion.

They are warriors.

This book is for you, the warriors of life. Follow the life of a shepherd boy who fought lions, killed bears, slew giants, and became a king.

Under shade trees tending sheep, the sweet psalmist of Israel had fellowship with the ultimate King Maker, God Himself.

Look deep into David's life and you will see your own reflection.

I offer this writing to you, my fellow warriors.

Section I

WARRIORS IN TRAINING

1

AN UNLIKELY WARRIOR

Leaders today would do well to model the heart of the second king of Israel, one who did not seek his own will, one who readily confessed sin and shortcomings, and one who allowed God to mold him into a powerful influence. David had a willing heart and willing hands, and he was willing to lead!

—Teresa Hampton[1]

But the Lord said to Samuel, "Do not consider his appearance or his height, for I have rejected him. The Lord does not look at the things people look at. People look at the outward appearance, but the Lord looks at the heart."

—1 Samuel 16:7

INTRODUCTION

The life of David is one of the most intriguing and inspiring studies in the Bible, apart from the life of Jesus. I don't know any other Bible character who has been written about as much as this man. There are 66 chapters (in the Bible) devoted to his life, along with 59 other Bible references. One would get the impression that his story is vital for us to study, and the lessons we can learn can serve us well, no matter our status in life.

David's name means "well-beloved." To coin a phrase, "he came from good stock."

- He was the son of Jesse, and Jesse was the grandson of Boaz and Ruth, so he was the great-grandson of Ruth and Boaz.
- He was a brilliant musician.
- He wrote some of the most beloved psalms and hymns.
- He became a fearless warrior.
- He was a priest to his people.
- He would eventually rule as king over a united Israel.
- He was the only person God declared in the Bible who was *"a man after my own heart"* (Acts 13:22).
- He is often seen in Old Testament theology as a "type" of Christ.

His wonderful attributes did not alter the fact that he was guilty of some of the most heinous sins one could commit. He took another man's wife and tried to cover it up by having her husband killed. He spent an enormous amount of time and energy trying to cover up his sins. David soon realized that he could cover up his sins for only so long, and he would eventually be exposed for all the kingdom to see!

There is an interesting verse of Scripture in 1 Kings 15:5. The Bible records this about David: *"For David had done what was right in the eyes of the Lord and had not failed to keep any of the Lord's commands all the days of his life—except in the case of Uriah the Hittite."* Did you catch that little phrase at the end? *"Except in the case of Uriah the Hittite."* God was bragging on David, and then He threw in that last line—I call it the "exception clause." I dare say that most (if not all) of us have an "exception clause" in our lives that we would like to forget.

David is an example of Numbers 32:23: *"But if you fail to do this, you will be sinning against the Lord; and you may be sure that your sin will find you out."* Do you think that when David did what he did he had any idea that movies would be made and books would be written about his supposedly secret sin? I doubt it. Even though horrible sins characterize his life, David is Exhibit A of God's grace and forgiveness. As all of us do, David sinned, but he confessed his sins and sought to restore his relationship with the Lord.

> David was a unique blending of soldier and shepherd, musician and military tactician, commander and commoner. In spite of his sins and failures—and we all have them—he was Israel's greatest king, and always will be until King Jesus reigns on David's throne as Prince of Peace. The next time we're tempted to emphasize the negative things in David's life, let's remember that Jesus wasn't ashamed to be called "the son of David."
>
> **—Warren W. Wiersbe**[2]

THE TIMES THEY ARE A-CHANGING

At the time of David's birth (around 1040 BC), Israel had turned their back on God. There had been a temporary revival under King Saul, but because of his disobedience God rejected him. Saul decided to do things his way and refused to listen to God's prophet. Remember, he only became king because Israel rejected the spiritual leadership of God mediated through the prophetic ministry of Samuel. Under the pressure of Philistine domination, the Israelites came to think that only a visible warrior-king could bring deliverance.

When young David was anointed king, Saul was still in power. Even though Saul was the people's choice to be king, God knew there would come a time when the cracks in his character would undo him. First Samuel 13:13-14 tells us:

> *"You have done a foolish thing," Samuel said. "You have not kept the command the Lord your God gave you; if you had, he would have established your kingdom over Israel for all time. But now your kingdom will not endure; the Lord has sought out a man after his own heart and appointed him ruler of his people, because you have not kept the Lord's command."*

What did Saul do that cost him his kingdom?

- He was greedy—1 Samuel 15:9
- He was disobedient—1 Samuel 15:8-9
- He was a man-pleaser—1 Samuel 15:24

- He blamed others for his sin—1 Samuel 15:13-21

And later, in 1 Samuel 16:1, we read, *"The Lord said to Samuel, 'How long will you mourn for Saul, since I have rejected him as king over Israel?'"*

"I have rejected Saul" is a terrifying statement! God's rejection of Saul was not yet evident to the people, and Saul was still putting up a front as the king. God's judgment did fall even though the people still believed Saul was the rightful king.

The kingdom was taken from Saul, and a new king was going to be anointed. It wasn't the popular choice. It was not going to be the most obvious choice—no, not at all! But it would be God's choice!

———•◆•◆•———

A TRUE UNDERDOG

Picture the scene.

It was time to anoint a new king. God told the prophet Samuel to go to the house of Jesse where he was given specific instructions: *"Fill your horn with oil and be on your way; I am sending you to Jesse of Bethlehem. I have chosen one of his sons to be king"* (1 Samuel 16:1). I don't know if Samuel thought this would be easy or not, but after reviewing Jesse's sons, he realized that God had a different standard than he did.

> *When they arrived, Samuel saw Eliab and thought, "Surely the Lord's anointed stands here before the Lord." But the*

Lord said to Samuel, "Do not consider his appearance or his height, for I have rejected him. The Lord does not look at the things people look at. People look at the outward appearance, but the Lord looks at the heart." Then Jesse called Abinadab and had him pass in front of Samuel. But Samuel said, "The Lord has not chosen this one either." Jesse then had Shammah pass by, but Samuel said, "Nor has the Lord chosen this one." Jesse had seven of his sons pass before Samuel, but Samuel said to him, "The Lord has not chosen these."

(1 Samuel 16:6-10)

Samuel looked at the eldest son, Eliab, and he was impressed with him. He must be "the one" because he's not only the oldest but also makes the most impressive appearance. *"When they arrived, Samuel saw Eliab and thought, 'Surely the Lord's anointed stands here before the Lord'"* (1 Samuel 16:6). But God rejected Eliab. Why?

But the Lord said to Samuel, "Do not consider his appearance or his height, for I have rejected him. The Lord does not look at the things people look at. People look at the outward appearance, but the Lord looks at the heart."

(1 Samuel 16:7)

Samuel was about to make the mistake of evaluating the sons of Jesse by their physical gifts (see 1 Samuel 10:24) when God reminded him the "heart of the matter" was a "matter of the heart."

As a rule, we tend to place more value on the outside, while God places more value on the inside. In our day, we judge people by how they look rather than act. We are guilty of failing to recognize that God can and does use all kinds of people who would never measure up to our standard.

The Bible is filled with men and women who had significant character flaws and were still used by God to accomplish great things.

- Abraham, the "father of the faithful" and a "friend of God," on occasion used deception to gain an advantage.
- Noah, the man who saved humanity, had a drinking problem.
- Moses murdered a man before he became a deliverer.
- Samson gave up his position as a judge for a prostitute.
- Peter was impulsive, prideful, and known to curse.
- Paul had blood on his hands and persecuted the Church.
- Timothy had ulcers and was fearful of his congregation.
- The apostles fell asleep in a prayer meeting.
- The woman at the well was married and divorced more than once.

Let's face it—we may judge someone as not usable simply because of how they look. God judges on another level and sees someone He can use to make a difference. We judge on appearance while God looks at a person's heart and sees a potential warrior. I have heard many people complain that they don't feel qualified for God's vision in their hearts.

They may say:

- I don't have enough education.

- I don't have the required skills.

- I don't have the finances.

- I don't have enough support from friends and family.

- I don't _____ (you fill in the blank).

It's time to start echoing the sentiment of the apostle Paul who said, *"I can do all this through him who gives me strength"* (Philippians 4:13). One lesson I've learned is God does not call the qualified, but He does qualify those He has called!

After God told Samuel that Eliab was not the one, the next son came in, and Samuel thought, *Surely this guy is the one.* Again, God said no. The rest of the sons lined up, and one by one, all were rejected.

> *Then Jesse called Abinadab and had him pass in front of Samuel. But Samuel said, "The Lord has not chosen this one either." Jesse then had Shammah pass by, but Samuel said, "Nor has the Lord chosen this one." Jesse had seven of his sons pass before Samuel, but Samuel said to him, "The Lord has not chosen these."*
>
> (1 Samuel 16:8-10)

Samuel had to figure that he either missed God or there was another son somewhere that he knew nothing about.

> *So he asked Jesse, "Are these all the sons you have?" "There is still the youngest," Jesse answered. "He is tending the sheep."*

Samuel said, "Send for him; we will not sit down until he arrives." So he sent for him and had him brought in. He was glowing with health and had a fine appearance and handsome features. Then the Lord said, "Rise and anoint him; this is the one."

(1 Samuel 16:11-12)

I have no idea what David thought while the church service was going on inside the house. I don't even know if David knew anything about what was going on. But I know what David was doing—he was out in the field tending his father's sheep.

In his book *David: A Man of Passion and Destiny,* Charles Swindoll writes:

Here's David, just a teenager. He walks into the house, still smelling like sheep, and all of a sudden an old man hobbles over and pours oil on his head. It drips down his hair and drops on his neck. Josephus the historian says that "Samuel the aged whispered in his ear the meaning of the symbol, 'you will be the next king.'"[3]

I cannot imagine the look on the faces of Jesse and his sons as they watched Samuel anoint young David. This was a private anointing, as David was not publicly anointed until he was 30 years old. It is unlikely that David or his family understood all the significance of the anointing that day.

In a day, in a single moment in time David, who was a nobody, became somebody. Author Travis Agnew said, "David was regarded as a nobody which made him a prime candidate to be used by God. Men saw his external, yet God saw his internal (1 Samuel 16:7). God anointed him for an incredible work and no one else saw it coming."[4]

WHAT CAN WE LEARN?

1. Don't Judge a Book by Its Cover

An old phrase says, "You can't judge a book by its cover." The meaning is obvious: one should not form an opinion on someone or something based purely on what is seen on the surface. After taking a deeper look, the person or thing may be very different than what was expected.

We all want to be somebody—that's a fact of the human experience. I don't know anyone who wants to be last in line or the last one picked. You may find yourself out in the pasture tending sheep (figuratively), wondering if anybody (besides a few family or friends) knows you're alive. David may have thought he would never amount to much more than a sheepherder, but God had other ideas.

As we shall soon see, David learned that being faithful in the mundane things of life can bring enormous blessings from the Lord. Jesus said if we can't be trusted with the little things, how can we be rewarded with bigger things?

Whoever can be trusted with very little can also be trusted with much, and whoever is dishonest with very little will also be dishonest with much. So if you have not been trustworthy in handling worldly wealth, who will trust you with true riches.

(Luke 16:10-11)

Samuel discovered that it's not always wise to go by appearances. Looking at someone's physical attributes doesn't always tell the story of what is on the inside.

2. Don't Listen to the Sheep

By sheep, I refer to *other people* who think they know what's best for your life. We all need friends and family to see potential in us, so we can accomplish great things and use our God-given talents and skills to rise above the crowd.

But the sad truth is there are times when those closest to us are the ones who will do everything in their power to "hold us back." It could be out of twisted fear that you might accomplish something they were afraid to try. The list is endless on why the sheep don't want you to leave the proverbial pasture. Make up your mind to never allow the sheep to determine your attitude or direction in life.

As we shall see (in a later chapter), when David steps up to fight Goliath, his brothers, along with King Saul, do everything to stop him from "making a fool out of himself." David had to learn quickly that there are times when the majority opinion will not be favorable, but press on anyway. There was nothing about David to suggest that he would sit on the throne one day, but God saw something in him that others didn't see—a humble heart turned toward Him.

3. Don't Run from the Underdog Label

I think we all would agree: David was a genuine underdog. Keep in mind when David's father called him "the youngest" in 1 Samuel 16:11 the word had more meaning than someone who was young in years. The expanded meaning of the word is that he was the lowest in his father's estimation—so little in his father's esteem that it wasn't necessary to include David when Samuel called the family to worship and offer sacrifice. Now that's a low blow!

Some of the world's most significant accomplishments were performed by the underdogs. Numerous examples from the world of sports recount how a nobody can become somebody almost overnight. None was more specular than the day a young man named Y.E. Yang took on the number-one golfer in the world, Tiger Woods.

Nick Dimengo writing for the Bleacher Report said,

> If there's one thing that 14-time major winner Tiger Woods typically does to opponents, it's intimidate them with his focus and intensity, especially when wearing his usual red shirt during the final round of a tournament. Unfortunately, that didn't happen for Woods in 2009's PGA Tournament. Then the No. 1 player in the world, Woods was upstaged by the guy ranked 110th, Y.E. Yang, who overcame a three-stroke lead in that last round to capture his first major title. Yang has only won two total

PGA tournaments in his career, but one of his wins came against the greatest golfer of the past 25 years.[5]

Your current circumstances are not a reliable indication of where you want to go. When David looked around, all he saw was another day hanging out with sheep, but God saw him as a warrior-king who would rule over a united Israel.

Pastor and author J.S. Park said it best:

> I always cheer when I read about David's anointing. Not because I have anything against his brothers. Not because of wish fulfillment for revenge-by-success. But because I have hope for guys like me. It's the same hope for you, too. A hope for those who have been left out, shoved to the back, and seen as second class.[6]

NOTES

1. Teresa Hampton, *Leading Ladies* (Big Cove, AL: Publishing Designs, Inc., 2001).

2. Warren W. Wiersbe. *The Wiersbe Bible Commentary: Old Testament* (Colorado Springs, CO: David Cook Publishing, 2007), 549.

3. Charles R. Swindoll, *David: A Man of Passion and Destiny* (Nashville, TN: Thomas Nelson, 2000), 35.

4. Travis Agnew, "When a Nobody Turns into Somebody," July 31, 2017, http://www.travisagnew.org/2017/07/31/when-a-nobody -turns-into-somebody.

5. Nick Dimengo, "Best Underdog Stories of the Past Decade," October 27, 2014, https://bleacherreport.com/articles/2243545 -best-underdog-stories-of-the-past-decade.

6. J.S. Park, *The Life of King David* (The Way Everlasting Ministry, 2015), 23.

2

JUST ANOTHER DAY WITH THE SHEEP

When God called David he was not out in the field preaching and teaching. David was being faithful in the "natural things." He didn't have any spiritual authority over anyone else, and he wasn't in Bible school. He was a good shepherd boy and a faithful son.

—Unknown

So Samuel took the horn of oil and anointed him in the presence of his brothers, and from that day on the Spirit of the Lord came powerfully upon David. Samuel then went to Ramah.

—1 Samuel 16:13

INTRODUCTION

What would you do if you had just been anointed king? Your hands are still dirty, there's mud on your boots, you stink of sheep, and yet the anointing oil (of a king) has stained your face. You know there has been a change in your circumstances, but how would it play out? Some people (no doubt) would clean up and head to the palace and start measuring for new curtains. Or maybe buy a new fleet of chariots. A newly anointed king could do plenty of things, but do you know what David did after Samuel anointed him? The same thing he'd been doing—tending his father's sheep!

David was a faithful son and not a self-promoter. Through his actions, his attitude becomes evident—he was content to remain where God planted him. Being king never entered David's mind, and I would imagine that being anointed king was as big a surprise to David as it was to anyone in his family. He was out in the pasture keeping his father's sheep, and, as far as I can tell, he never complained about the most menial task a son could perform.

David's faithfulness in the mundane things would soon be rewarded as he would be summoned to the palace to play music for the king. Notice the contrast between Saul and David: the Spirit came upon David but departed from Saul (see 1 Samuel 16:13-14).

Saul's servants were mindful that the king was troubled by an evil spirit. They felt the only relief for the king was to find a skilled musician to play music to soothe his tortured soul

> Saul's attendants said to him, "See, an evil spirit from God is tormenting you. Let our lord command his servants here to search for someone who can play the lyre. He will play when the evil spirit from God comes on you, and you will feel better."
>
> (1 Samuel 16:15-16)

To all appearances, David was just the man Saul needed. As I said earlier, he was not a self-promoter. God was the one opening doors for David that he could never open for himself. Proverbs 22:29 says, *"Do you see someone skilled in their work? They will serve before kings; they will not serve before officials of low rank."* And Proverbs 18:16 says, *"A gift opens the way and ushers the giver into the presence of the great."*

David was a big hit in the king's court. But that didn't last long. I have no doubt if Saul had known that God chose David to be king, he would have had David killed.

At this point in David's life, three questions need to be asked:

WOULD GOD CHOOSE TO USE A NOBODY LIKE DAVID?

The basis of how God chooses someone is not at all what we think. God's standards are worlds apart from how we choose our leaders. The apostle Paul gave some of the best insight into the matter when he wrote his first letter to the Corinthian believers.

The Lord does not choose someone because he is intelligent, influential, or has a high standing in the social world (see 1 Corinthians 1:26). That is not to say that He never calls anyone who is intelligent, influential, or has a high standing in the social world, but according to Paul just not many.

What is God's standard? In 1 Corinthians 1:26-31, Paul shared how God chooses leaders:

Brothers and sisters, think of what you were when you were called. Not many of you were wise by human standards; not many were influential; not many were of noble birth. But God chose the foolish things of the world to shame the wise; God chose the weak things of the world to shame the strong. God chose the lowly things of this world and the despised things—and the things that are not—to nullify the things that are, so that no one may boast before him. It is because of him that you are in Christ Jesus, who has become for us wisdom from God—that is, our righteousness, holiness and redemption. Therefore, as it is written: "Let the one who boasts boast in the Lord."

May I give you my interpretation of what Paul said? God does the choosing, and He can take anyone—regardless of influence, education, or social standing—to bring about His purposes. God picks the nobodies and will showcase them to confound a world that needs to see His glory upon the earth! God is not necessarily looking for showboats, superstars, or high-powered ministers to get the job done. God chooses those who will reflect His glory!

Please don't misunderstand; I am grateful for every prominent person who is not ashamed to speak for their faith. But for every Tim Tebow, Denzel Washington, Tyler Perry, MC Hammer, or Carrie Underwood (and more), countless others (the nobodies) will never be famous or recognized but are just as influential for the cause of Christ.

Ida Tarbell...was asked on her 80th birthday to name the greatest people she had ever met, and she replied, "Those nobody knows anything about." Some of the greatest and famous people in the history book of God are obscure nobodies in the history books of men. Sometimes it happens that obscurity is a blessing because it leaves a person free to give their life in service rather than in display.[1]

If I were making a list of those who belonged in God's *Nobodies Hall of Fame,* it would have included the two fellows below:

Moses

For the first forty years of his life, Moses learned how to be a somebody and would be known as the "Prince of Egypt." But in the second forty years of his life, Moses learned how to be a nobody on the back side of the desert herding sheep. The prince everyone thought would become the next ruler of Egypt became a pauper, a simple nobody. But in the last forty years of his life, Moses learned that God can take a nobody and make him into a somebody who would become God's prophet to the nation and lead them out of captivity.

Gideon

God wanted to use Gideon as a mighty judge to deliver the people from their bondage. When the Lord caught up with him, he was hiding in a winepress, scared like a little child. I love how the angel of the Lord approached him: *"When the angel of the Lord appeared to Gideon, he said, 'The Lord is with you, mighty warrior'"* (Judges 6:12). I can almost see Gideon looking around and saying, "Are you sure you have the right guy?" The Lord paid no attention to Gideon's words or fears and said, *"Go in the strength you have and save Israel out of Midian's hand. Am I not sending you?"* (Judges 6:14). God took a nobody and turned him into somebody who would take 300 men and rout the entire army of the Midianites!

What about you? Do you feel unqualified to accomplish great things? Do you see yourself like Moses on the back side of the desert or Gideon hiding from the enemy? When we stand before the Lord, we won't be bragging about our education, money, or how our powerful friends got us there. God uses us not because of our ability but because of our availability. If God can make a donkey talk, think of what He can do with us! (Read Numbers 22:26-30.)

So back to the first question: why does God choose to use nobodies? It's not hard to understand: *"so that no one may boast before him"* (1 Corinthians 1:29). Whatever success we have or victories gained, it's all because of our availability and dependence on His power working through us.

> *I know what it is to be in need, and I know what it is to have plenty. I have learned the secret of being content in any and every situation, whether well fed or hungry, whether living in plenty or in want. I can do all this through him who gives me strength.*
>
> (Philippians 4:12-13)

Why Is Faithfulness over "Little Things" so Important?

When we realize that God wants to use us for His glory, we sometimes have the idea that the natural or little things of a daily routine are of no importance. While the anointing oil was still wet on David's head, he went back to doing what he was assigned to do. He didn't run out to the pasture to start a television ministry with a product table and put together a complete mailing list of donors. That didn't happen!

An all-too-familiar refrain among believers is, "Going to work, paying bills, and cutting grass are not so important anymore because I have a calling from God. I don't have time to do those mundane things because I'm going to do great things in the Kingdom of God." It's doing the little things that makes it possible to do more extraordinary things in the future.

Faithfulness in the little things will test your integrity.

Rick Warren observed that our integrity is tested in the little things of life.

> God uses little things to test your integrity. We think it's the big things in life that create a leader—but no. The big crisis in life reveal leadership, but leadership is not built in the big things of life. It's built in the small things. That's where integrity shows up—in the stuff that nobody sees, in the stuff behind the scenes, and in the small, unseen, unspectacular choices of life where you do the right thing

even though nobody's ever going to see it. Faithfulness requires integrity, and God tests your integrity in the little things. In Luke 16:10 Jesus says, *"Whoever is faithful in small matters will be faithful in large ones; whoever is dishonest in small matters will be dishonest in large ones"* (GNT). He's saying your public blessing is determined by your private integrity.[2]

Faithfulness (stewardship) in the little things will gain you trust for bigger things.

Did you know that Jesus talked about stewardship (money) in 16 of 38 parables? And there are 500 verses on prayer and 2,000 on possessions. Jesus loved to use illustrations when it came to our stewardship.

Jesus used illustrations of *stewards* (Matthew 25:14-30; Luke 16:1-13) and *farming* (Matthew 13:8,23; John 4:34-38). He taught "that it is appropriate, and even expected by the Lord, to invest our resources for long-term gain and/or financial security. ...Jesus taught that, since we are merely stewards, we should invest ourselves into the lives of others, not hoard our resources for ourselves (Matthew 25:34-40; Luke 6:30-38; 10:25-37; 12:15-21)."[3]

Jesus made it abundantly clear there is a direct correlation between how I handle the little things and whether or not I can be trusted with more important things. In the parable in Luke 16, He's referring to our stewardship of "things."

Whoever can be trusted with very little can also be trusted with much, and whoever is dishonest with very little will also be dishonest with much. So if you have not been trustworthy in handling worldly wealth, who will trust you with true riches? And if you have not been trustworthy with someone else's property, who will give you property of your own? No one can serve two masters. Either you will hate the one and love the other, or you will be devoted to the one and despise the other. You cannot serve both God and money.

(Luke 16:10-13)

The real issue is a matter of trust. Can the Lord trust me to give proper stewardship to what I have? Trust is not a gift of the Spirit—it's earned, and it can be broken. Why would God give us more if we misuse what we already have? And it's not just about money here. If I can't be trusted to manage my time, talents, relationships, and treasure, then I cannot be trusted with more. What you have *right now* is as much as you can be trusted to manage!

The bottom line is fairly simple: if He can't trust us with very little, then we can't be trusted with very much. Before we decide that doing the little things is beneath us, we might want to stop and consider how God measures trust. If we have been faithful in a few things, we will get *more*—if not, what we have may be taken away! (See Matthew 21:28-31; Mark 4:24-25.) Trust is never measured by what we are planning to do but by what actions we are taking right now—today!

Faithfulness in the little things will serve as a stepping stone for promotion.

Before David met Goliath on the battlefield, he left his responsibilities tending sheep to be a messenger for his father:

> *Now Jesse said to his son David, "Take this ephah of roasted grain and these ten loaves of bread for your brothers and hurry to their camp. Take along these ten cheeses to the commander of their unit. See how your brothers are and bring back some assurance from them."*
>
> (1 Samuel 17:17-18)

It may not have seemed like a big deal at the time, but David's straightforward act of obedience put him in a position to become a hero to the nation of Israel. He could have said, "I need to pray about it," or "Send somebody else; I don't have time." But he didn't—and we all know the rest of the story.

Here is a principle at work: David's obedience and faithfulness were the foundation stones for his next promotion. He would have never met and defeated Goliath had he not obeyed the voice of his father and been faithful to fulfill a simple task—take your brothers food and see how they are doing. It doesn't get any more mundane than that, yet the rewards of his obedience changed his life forever!

It's easy to forget how important everyday life is. When work is mundane, when we are given assignments below our skill level, when we feel stuck in the daily grind—we sometimes forget that everyday life is the training ground for greatness. —Leif Hetland[4]

AM I WILLING TO WAIT ON GOD FOR PROMOTION?

While David was tending sheep, God was shaping his character. For fourteen years, he was taught on the backside of nowhere. David's faithfulness allowed him to become the person God could use. You see, everyone God uses will have to learn the lesson of *waiting*. It's the most difficult thing for most of us to do. I hate to break it to you, but in shaping our character God doesn't use a microwave; He uses a crockpot.

Noah waited 120 years while building the Ark. Moses waited 40 years while he took care of a bunch of stinking sheep. The Israelites waited 400 years in Egypt before they were delivered. Abraham waited until he was 100 years old for Isaac. Jesus waited 30 years before His ministry began. God uses people who are willing to wait, not knowing how long they will have to wait.

While David was out in the field, he was anointed king yet had no subjects or kingdom to rule. Interestingly, rather than complain or pout, he worshiped and sang. During all his "shepherd time," he was connecting with the Lord, living in His presence. Young David was unlike many church folks who don't get their way. He had no Bible to read and no explanations from God. He was being faithful. Years later, an older David wrote, *"Wait for the Lord; be strong and take heart and wait for the*

Lord" (Psalm 27:14), and later declared, *"I wait for the Lord, my whole being waits, and in his word I put my hope"* (Psalm 130:5).

J.I. Packer observed:

> Wait on the Lord is a constant refrain in the Psalms, and it is a necessary word, for God often keeps us waiting. He is not in such a hurry as we are, and it is not his way to give more light on the future than we need for action in the present, or to guide us more than one step at a time. When in doubt, do nothing, but continue to wait on God. When action is needed, light will come.[5]

Let's be honest—waiting on anything is not our strong suit. This generation is about "give it to me now," not tomorrow or next week—but now! But we must understand that God is about *timing*, not time. He doesn't look at calendars or watches as much as we may think.

If we are willing to trust God in the process and not run ahead, we will see great things. A failure to wait on the Lord will always produce a counterfeit, as seen in the life of Abraham. God wants us to avoid producing an Ishmael. Nothing good ever comes from running ahead of the Lord. Instead of Ishmael, God wants to give us an Isaac—but we must learn to wait on His timing (see Genesis 16–18).

———————◆·◆·◆———————

What Can We Learn?

1. God Loves to Use Nobodies

Why does the Lord choose nobodies when plenty of so-called famous people are dying for the spotlight? It is relatively simple—to show the world that He only needs a willing vessel to demonstrate His glory. And He will qualify those whom He has called (see 1 Corinthians 1:26-31).

2. The Importance of Being Faithful in the Mundane Things

God emphasizes faithfulness, obedience, and availability above money, natural ability, and social standing. He is not looking for superstars, big-shots, and television personalities to advance the kingdom.

3. Waiting on God Is Necessary but Can Be Difficult

Waiting on the Lord is a necessary part of the "training for reigning" process. Teacher and author Joshua Infantado said, "His plans are greater than your greatest disappointments. Yes, waiting can be tough at times, but it is through waiting that we develop patience, endurance, and faith. So, be at peace. God is working something that is greater than anything you'll ever know!"[6]

NOTES

1. Glenn Pease, "How to Be a Successful Nobody," https://sermons
   .faithlife.com/sermons/125072-how-to-be-a-successful-nobody.

2. Rick Warren, "Being Faithful in the Little Things," April 28, 2018,
   https://pastorrick.com/devotional/english/being-faithful-in-the
   -little-things.

3. Father Okwuosa, "9 Things Jesus Actually Taught About Money,"
   June 13, 2018, https://www.arkofgreatness.org/2018/06/9-things
   -jesus-actually-taught-about.html.

4. Leif Hetland, *Giant Slayers* (Shippensburg, PA: Destiny Image,
   2017), 27.

5. J.I. Packer, *Knowing God* (Downers Grove, IL: InterVarsity Press,
   1973), 82.

6. Joshua Infantado, "Don't Run Ahead of God," November 6, 2019,
   https://becomingchristians.com/2019/11/06/dont-run-ahead-of
   -god.

3

WHAT EVERY WARRIOR
WILL FACE

*Any fool can criticize, complain, and condemn—and most fools
do. But it takes character and self-control to be understanding
and forgiving.*

—Dale Carnegie[1]

*When Eliab, David's oldest brother, heard him speaking with
the men, he burned with anger at him and asked, "Why have
you come down here? And with whom did you leave those few
sheep in the wilderness? I know how conceited you are and how
wicked your heart is; you came down only to watch the battle."
"Now what have I done?" said David. "Can't I even speak?"*

—1 Samuel 17:28-29

INTRODUCTION

U nder the maxim "no good deed goes unpunished," it's not surprising that David's presence generated an adverse reaction when he reached the battlefield. Keep in mind that David would be the only one—and I repeat, the only one—willing to face Goliath. Yet before he ever picked up the five smooth stones to take out the "giant problem," he was severely challenged by some unexpected sources. Instead of words of encouragement, he was accused, criticized, and maligned.

I don't care what leadership level you've attained; at some point, you will face similar circumstances. You try to lead with a positive attitude and make sure those around you are successful, and yet there will be those who think they can do a better job than you.

On April 23, 1910, Theodore Roosevelt gave a speech at the Sorbonne in Paris, France. He made the following observation about critics:

> It is not the critic who counts, not the man who points out how the strong man stumbled, or where the doer of deeds could have done better. The credit belongs to the man who is actually in the arena; whose face is marred by the dust and sweat and blood; who strives valiantly; who errs and comes short again and again, because there is no effort without error or shortcoming; who knows the great enthusiasms, the great devotions and spends himself in a worthy cause; who at the best, knows in the end the triumph of high achievement, and who, at worst, if he fails, at least fails while daring greatly; so that his place

shall never be with those cold and timid souls who know neither victory or defeat.[2]

What Roosevelt said in 1910 is just as relevant today. Critics have always been with us, like the flu, but that doesn't make it any less annoying!

David was slowly transforming from a shepherd boy to a warrior-king, but it was not without a price. There was a warrior inside of David, a champion giant killer, but before he ever took the field of battle, he had to dig deep inside and realize not everyone was on the sidelines cheering on his success.

There is always a price to pay for greatness—no exceptions. History is filled with examples of men and women who overcame obstacles to rise to the level of a champion.

For instance, Usain Bolt became known as the fastest man in the world. But it took an "I will not quit attitude" and a massive amount of hard work to achieve his goal. He was willing to pay the price, including physical and mental challenges.

Tuomas Haapssari shared the following:

> In 1996 when Usain Bolt watched the Atlanta Olympics 100 meter finals, he decided to be the fastest man in the world someday. After his decision he has spent all his time and energy training and competing.
>
> In his twenties he was diagnosed with severe scoliosis. The doctor said that he could probably never compete again.

He didn't give up and found a way to keep his back in good condition.

In 2015 Bolt raced against Justin Gatlin in Peking Olympic Games 100m finals. The starting point was this: Gatlin was in his best ever physical condition. He had won all the competitions during the season. Bolt was not in a very good condition. He had had lots of back problems. The expectation was that Gatlin would conquer Bolt.

In the semifinals Gatlin was clearly the fastest. Bolt was close to ruining his semifinal run by almost falling in the start. He was still able to make it to the finals. Finals started well for both Gatlin and Bolt. Gatlin was leading the race until 90 meters when his running broke down and Bolt got ahead of him. Bolt kept his position till the end and won the race by one hundredth of a second! His winning time was worse than Gatlin's semifinal time but still just good enough for the victory.[3]

Yes, David became a champion, a giant killer, but before he celebrated the rewards of killing Goliath, he had to overcome an unexpected obstacle.

Big Brother Knows Best

When Eliab, David's oldest brother, heard him speaking with the men, he burned with anger at him and asked, "Why have you come down here? And with whom did you leave those few sheep in the wilderness? I know how conceited you are and how wicked your heart is; you came down only to watch the battle." "Now what have I done?" said David. "Can't I even speak?" He then turned away to someone else and brought up the same matter, and the men answered him as before.

(1 Samuel 17:28-30)

It was not a random soldier or an aid to the king who "opened up" on David. Eliab, his older brother, gave David sharp and unnecessary criticism. We would have never guessed that a family member would be the first to launch a frontal assault on David. For generations, there has been an unspoken rule among brothers: *the older brother is to take care of the younger brother.* But listening to Eliab talk to David, it's evident that he thinks the rule does not apply to him!

It has been suggested that Eliab was concerned that David would get himself killed. In other words, he was trying to shame David into forgetting any idea of facing off against Goliath, but I can't entirely agree with that analysis. Something else was going on.

What do you suppose was going on with Eliab that caused him to react to David in such a cruel way? Looking back at 1 Samuel 16, it was Eliab whom everyone (including Samuel) expected to be anointed king. David was tending sheep and was not invited to join the family to meet with the prophet. I doubt David knew what was happening in the house until his father called for him. Eliab was Samuel's choice—but not God's. First Samuel 16:6-7 tells us:

> *When they arrived, Samuel saw Eliab and thought, "Surely the Lord's anointed stands here before the Lord." But the Lord said to Samuel, "Do not consider his appearance or his height, for I have rejected him. The Lord does not look at the things people look at. People look at the outward appearance, but the Lord looks at the heart."*

It was to be David, not Eliab. And that might give us insight into what was going on in the conversation between the two brothers.

It must have been a shock to David to realize that not everyone would cheer on his vision or root for his success. Eliab heard David asking questions, which put him into a full-blown meltdown. David didn't make his brother mad—his brother was angry already. All David did was expose the anger in Eliab's heart. Like squeezing a tube of toothpaste, what's inside will come out when enough pressure is applied.

David must have thought, *Here I am obeying my father, and all I get for my trouble is grief!* Eliab was so jealous of David's courage that he fell into the trap of criticizing what he didn't understand.

At the heart of Eliab's criticism were three accusations:

WHAT EVERY WARRIOR WILL FACE

First, He accused David of pride. *"I know how conceited you are, and how wicked your heart is."* Eliab developed x-ray vision, looked into David's heart, and determined he was full of pride. When a critic can't find any other way to bring you down, they will always impugn your motives.

Second, he accused David of neglecting his responsibility. *"And with whom did you leave those few sheep in the desert?"* Eliab was saying, "You should be a good little boy and go back and take care of the sheep; you have no business here."

Third, he accused David of a wicked curiosity. *"You came down only to watch the battle."* No matter what David said, it was going to be wrong. Instead of trying to reason with his brother, he turned away and started talking to the others who were standing around.

David's heart was stirred, and bold courage began to bubble up out of his spirit. He knew that shrinking back and hiding from the enemy would only lead to humiliation, destruction, defeat, and enslavement.

Why did David face such sharp criticism? There could be many reasons. I don't know all of them, but let me suggest a few.

He Was Too Young

David was indeed young and inexperienced in the way of war. But Eliab knew that David had been anointed king, and he didn't like it.

Some people are like water boys on a football team. They wait until you look like you're "getting hot," and then they want to throw water in your face. There will always be those waiting on your success so that they can be around to cool you off when you're getting too far ahead.

History is filled with young people who didn't allow their age to stop them from accomplishing great things. Below are four of my favorites from an article entitled "6 Teenagers Who Made History":

- *Joan of Arc*: Despite having no military experience, she led the French army in a major victory against the English at Orleans during the Hundred Years' war at the young age of 13.

- *Bobby Fischer*: In 1958, at age 15, Bobby Fischer became the youngest chess player in history to be named grandmaster, the highest title possible.

- *Louis Braille*: The Braille language for the blind was developed by Louis Braille in 1824, when he was just 15 years old. He tweaked it and expanded it after that, but, having been blind himself since the age of 3, he was inspired at a young age to conceive of a way to read and write.

- *Malala Yousafzai*: In 2014, at age 17, Malala Yousafzai became the youngest recipient of the Nobel Peace Prize. The young activist from Pakistan had become famous for speaking out against the Taliban and encouraging young girls like herself to pursue an education. She made her first public speech touting the cause when she was only 11 years old. She attracted international attention when she survived an attempt on her life at age 15.[4]

Anybody but Him

It is apparent from reading 1 Samuel 16 that David was not the first choice to be king. He was not even on the list in the mind of his family. They must've thought, "Anybody but him."

It's called the "lead dog" principle. You know the old saying, "If you're not the lead dog, the view never changes." There will always be others who think they can do a better job, so they are always heaping criticism on you. It's always something—you're too young, or too old, or you don't have enough education; you haven't been on the job long enough or you haven't paid "your dues." You name it and the critics will come up with some reason to negate you.

It Should Be Me!

The pain and embarrassment of not being chosen king must have been overwhelming for Eliab. How Eliab must have felt when he realized he was *not* going to be anointed king. It would be like expecting to be selected first in the NBA draft only to find out you were not even drafted. We're talking about a severe blow to one's ego. And to make matters worse, to have your younger brother selected and anointed king instead of you!

I didn't see anyone stopping Eliab, or any of David's brothers, from strapping on their armor and going out to meet Goliath. David represented a new breed of leader who was willing to put his faith in God's Word and not be swayed by fear or criticism. Neither Eliab's criticism nor Saul's refusal to fight kept David from believing God for the victory.

WHAT CAN WE LEARN?

1. The Critics Will Always Be among Us

If you haven't figured it out by now, you will—criticism is a fact of life. You can run from it, hide under your bed, and hope it will disappear, but it never does.

Remember, you can't eliminate the critic, but you can work on your attitude. Correction can come in many shapes and sizes. Sometimes it may even come from someone you don't like or respect. Whether it comes from a family member, like Eliab, or someone you don't know very well—attitude is everything!

Our first reaction is usually wrong. We defend ourselves. Sometimes we even lash back. It's a natural thing to do. Once we get over our wounded pride, we can sit down and take inventory to see if there is any truth to what we heard. Proverbs 16:32 tells us, *"Better a patient person than a warrior, one with self-control than one who takes a city."*

Here are a few guidelines for dealing with criticism:

- Take a deep breath and give it a little thought. Ask the Lord enter your thoughts.
- Don't overreact. Choose to respond rather than retaliate.

- Consider the source. It's always best to see beyond the present situation—just as we looked at Eliab's deeper reasons for resentment.

- Try turning a negative into a positive. Remember "soft answers turn away wrath."

- Make something useful out of the criticism. Check yourself. Is there something the other person is seeing about you that you missed?

- Heap coals of fire on their head—bless them, don't curse them.

- Make positive, faith-filled people a part of your inner circle.

2. Focus on Your Purpose (the Giant) Instead of the Critics

You will notice that David didn't take time to debate his brother. He heard what Eliab had to say and replied:

> *"Now what have I done?" said David. "Can't I even speak?"*
> *He then turned away to someone else and brought up the*
> *same matter, and the men answered him as before.*

(1 Samuel 17:29-30)

David met this charge in the very wisest way—he answered with a few soft words, and then turned away. He did not continue to argue, for in such a contest, to multiply words is to increase ill feelings and he who is silent first is the conqueror. Grandly did this young man restrain himself, though the provocation was very severe, and herein he won the honors of the man who restrains his spirit and greater than the soldier who takes a city. I admire David as he selects his five smooth stones from the brook, but I admire him quite as much when he so gently replies where others might have been angry—and then so wisely turns aside from a debate which could not have been to the profit of either party.[5]

3. No One Is Immune

As I said earlier, it doesn't matter what level of leadership you have attained; you will never be out of the reach of negative-minded people who want to bring you down a notch or two. Anyone who has ever accomplished anything worthwhile has faced the sharp knife of criticism. The most remarkable men and women of the Bible and human history were criticized, accused, and maligned. So cheer up, you're in good company when it happens to you.

Elbert G. Hubbard (1856–1915) was a renowned American philosopher, artist, and publisher. It would not be a mischaracterization to call him a marketing genius; he is considered by many to be the grandfather of marketing. Along with his success came criticism—heaps of criticism. In November 1909, he said:

If a man is alive, if he's tapping the reservoirs, he is sure to meet defeat. He'll be knocked, he'll be misunderstood, laughed at and perhaps called a foe to society.

For the man who doesn't want to be knocked and laughed at I give this recipe: Do nothing, say nothing, be nothing. Go in your hole and pull your hole after you and put up a sign "not at home." If any man follows this recipe, I assure you, he will never get turned down.[6]

We all have our Eliabs who are more willing to tell us what *not* to do. Then, when we try to do the right thing, they stand over our shoulder and criticize our every word.

The truth is they never seem to get in the game themselves, and they don't want you to be successful. David ignored the critics and focused on his assignments.

We can do the same by allowing the Holy Spirit to give us the wisdom and insight to follow David's example.

NOTES

1. Dale Carnegie, *How to Win Friends and Influence People* (Sinom & Schuster, 1936), 36.

2. Theodore Roosevelt, "Citizenship in a Republic," Speech, Paris, France, April 23, 1910.

3. Tuomas Haapsaari, "How to Awaken the Champion Within You: 3 Inspirational Stories," accessed June 11, 2022, https://www.zef .fi/blog/how-to-awaken-the-champion-within-you-3-inspirational -stories.

4. Naomi Blumberg, "6 Teenagers Who Made History," Britannica
    .com https://www.britannica.com/story/6-teenagers-who-made
    -history.

5. C.H. Spurgeon, "The Lion-slayer—the Giant-killer," Sermon, The
    Metropolitan Tabernacle, Newington, September 5, 1875, https://
    ccel.org/ccel/spurgeon/sermons21/sermons21.xliv.html.

6. *Cleveland Plain Dealer*, "Hubbard Praises Mayor Johnson:
    The Fra, Here on Lecture Bent," November 7, 1909, https://
    quoteinvestigator.com/2015/01/09/say-nothing.

4

IN THE VALLEY OF ELAH

Get the right perspective. When Goliath came against the Israelites, the soldiers all thought, "He is so big. We can never kill him." David looked at the same giant and thought, "He is so big. I can't miss."

—Russell Johnston[1]

Now Jesse said to his son David, "Take this ephah of roasted grain and these ten loaves of bread for your brothers and hurry to their camp. Take along these ten cheeses to the commander of their unit. See how your brothers are and bring back some assurance from them. They are with Saul and all the men of Israel in the Valley of Elah, fighting against the Philistines."

—1 Samuel 17:17-19

INTRODUCTION

Without exception, we will be tested. As the saying goes, "We are either facing a test now, just came through one, or we are about to face a new one." It's a slice of cold comfort to realize that spiritual maturity, social standing, or education eliminates the possibility of facing off against a giant.

Some tests are easily overcome, and we move on. Some tests are more complex, but we prevail and live to fight another day. For instance, in the previous chapter we saw how David handled the test of *criticism, discouragement, and fear,* but there comes a time when the "mother of all tests" shows up. We stand there with our knees knocking, frozen in fear, all the while wondering, "Where in the world did this come from?" It may be a marital problem, a health problem, a financial meltdown, or whatever name you want; everyone will face a giant sooner or later. They may not all be over nine feet tall, but trust me, when facing one, things may appear impossible. John Newton said that "Trials are medicines which our gracious and wise physician prescribes because we need them; and he proportions the frequency and weight of them to what the case requires."[2]

Here is David, taking care of his father's sheep and minding his own business when he is thrust headlong into a life-changing experience. He was comfortable. He had a part-time job at the palace—and spent the rest of the time perfecting his composing skills by singing to his congregation (the herd of sheep).

The account of David and Goliath is one of the more familiar stories in the Bible. It is filled with many practical applications, and none are more critical than recognizing no matter how big our giant appears, *we can overcome it by the power of God!*

There's a Battle Brewing

First Samuel 17:1-3 sets the scene:

> *Now the Philistines gathered their forces for war and assembled at Sokoh in Judah. They pitched camp at Ephes Dammim, between Sokoh and Azekah. Saul and the Israelites assembled and camped in the Valley of Elah and drew up their battle line to meet the Philistines. The Philistines occupied one hill and the Israelites another, with the valley between them.*

Above the ridges of the Elah Valley, the two armies were faced off—on one side were the Philistines, and on the other were the Israelites led by King Saul. Neither army dared to attack, as that would mean making the dangerous gamble to leave a position of strength and descend into the valley to then attack the side occupying the high ground—foolhardy at best and suicidal at worst. Thus, both armies stood their ground, waiting and watching each other.

Finally, the Philistines had enough of waiting for the army of Saul to make their move. Goliath stepped out—a giant problem for Saul and his army.

> *Goliath stood and shouted to the ranks of Israel, "Why do you come out and line up for battle? Am I not a Philistine, and are you not the servants of Saul? Choose a man and have him come down to me. If he is able to fight and kill me,*

we will become your subjects; but if I overcome him and kill him, you will become our subjects and serve us." Then the Philistine said, "This day I defy the armies of Israel! Give me a man and let us fight each other." On hearing the Philistine's words, Saul and all the Israelites were dismayed and terrified.

(1 Samuel 17:8-11)

Every morning the Philistines trotted out their champion, Goliath, to challenge Saul's army. Just the mention of the name *Goliath* brought paralyzing fear. He was no ordinary warrior. The consensus among Bible teachers is that he stood around nine feet, nine inches tall; his armor consisted of a bronze helmet, a coat of scale armor weighing over one hundred twenty-five pounds, and a pair of bronze leggings. His weapons were a bronze spear with a fifteen-pound tip, a sword, and a javelin. His shield was carried by an armor-bearer who walked before him. He was trained to kill, not compromise with his enemy: "kill me, or I'll kill you" was his war cry!

On the surface, this was not going to be a fair fight. Historians tell us that the height of an average man in that day was around 5 feet 2 inches tall. There were exceptions like Saul, who was "head and shoulders" above his brethren, but for the most part this was going to be a slaughter for whoever the Israelites sent out to fight him.

In those days, they had an unusual rule of combat. They would send out their most able warriors to fight each other in order to prevent unnecessary loss of life. This duel would be a representative war with the loser's nation becoming subject to the winner, serving the winning nation as slaves. The outcome was thought to be the judgment of the gods on the matter. Thus, the fight was between the Philistines' gods and the God of Israel.

Day after day, Goliath would challenge the army to send out a man to fight. *"Then the Philistine said, 'This day I defy the armies of Israel! Give me a man and let us fight each other'"* (1 Samuel 17:10).

On the other side of the ravine was an army that refused to fight— hiding in their foxholes, shaking in fear. Why did Saul's army line up to fight when not a single soldier would go out to face him? The logical choice to face Goliath would have been Saul. He was the king and had every right to call upon the God of Israel to defend his army.

The fear of Goliath paralyzed Saul, so he was in no position to lead the army into battle. Had Saul been the anointed and godly leader he was supposed to be, he would've claimed the assurance of God's presence fighting for them to lead his troops to victory:

When you go to war against your enemies and see horses and chariots and an army greater than yours, do not be afraid of them, because the Lord your God, who brought you up out of Egypt, will be with you. When you are about to go into battle, the priest shall come forward and address the army. He shall say: "Hear, Israel: Today you are going into battle against your enemies. Do not be fainthearted or afraid; do not panic or be terrified by them. For the Lord your God is the one who goes with you to fight for you against your enemies to give you victory."

(Deuteronomy 20:1-4)

But soon, there would be a young man who would take on the giant. His name would go down in history as the one who took down Goliath. He would become known as David: GGK (Great Giant Killer).

———◆•◆•◆———

THE BATTLE IS JOINED

David's day started like any other. When he dressed that morning and headed out to the pasture, I doubt that he thought this was *not* going to be anything other than an ordinary day. You know, just another day with the sheep.

Maybe he knew a battle was going on (or not), but what did that have to do with him? Occasionally, his father, Jesse, would send him on an errand to the front lines to check on his brothers. He was too young to be thinking that this fight with the Philistines was any of his affair. David didn't know it yet, but this day *was* going to be different.

Many of us have discovered that life-changing experiences don't usually come knocking on our door dressed up as "life-changing experiences." Instead, they come unannounced, disguised as ordinary assignments that challenge us to remain faithful to our calling no matter how insignificant the assignments appear.

What Did David Do?

He showed up!

David's assignment was simple: Jesse told him to *"Go take food and check on your brothers."* He could have said yes and wandered off somewhere else, distracted by other things. He could have thought to himself, *This assignment is too dangerous,* or *It's a waste of time,* or whatever excuse he could've come up with for not being obedient to his father.

He didn't do that—he obeyed his father's wishes.

One of the most essential *abilities* one can have is *dependability.* It's the attitude of "I can be counted on no matter the assignment." Neal Maxwell said, "God does not begin by asking us about our ability, but only about our availability, and if we then prove our dependability, he will increase our capability."[3]

Half the battle is already won when you show up where you're supposed to be. You may not win all the battles all the time, but I promise you will lose all the battles all the time if you don't show up.

What Did David Say?

Day after day, morning and evening, Goliath defied the army. *"For forty days the Philistine came forward every morning and evening and took his stand"* (1 Samuel 17:16). Every time these big, tough, hardened soldiers heard Goliath's challenge, they would run and hide like frightened rabbits! King Saul did everything he could to encourage his frightened soldiers to fight. He sent out a text alert that read: "Any soldier who will take on Goliath and kill him will receive unlimited wealth, my beautiful daughter in marriage, and tax exemption for himself and his entire family." He put them on the "incentive" plan, but even that didn't work.

But today was going to be different. When David heard the challenge of Goliath, something stirred in his spirit. David uttered his first recorded words:

> *David asked the men standing near him, "What will be done for the man who kills this Philistine and removes this disgrace from Israel? Who is this uncircumcised Philistine that he should defy the armies of the living God?"*
>
> (1 Samuel 17:26)

You can see the difference between fear and faith by how Saul's army and David responded to Goliath.

Saul's army said, "Goliath is too big to hit!"

David shouted, "Goliath is too big to miss!"

No fight in history has been chronicled more than David and Goliath—not even the infamous fight between Tyson and Holyfield in June 1997 or the "Thrilla in Manila" between Ali and Frazier in 1975. Many others captured the nation's attention, but the fight between David and Goliath outranks them all for the sheer drama. Usually, when two men face off in the ring, they are fighting for the gold and the glory; but when these two men faced off on the field of battle (in representative combat), entire nations hung in the balance.

Everything was against David. His brothers scorned him, Saul discouraged him, and Goliath mocked him. But David determined that Goliath had to go—and he was just the man to handle the job.

When the king realized that David was their only hope, he tried to give David his armor. David refused. Instead, he would use what had already been proven while watching over his sheep. His weapons were good enough to kill the lion and the bear. And now he would demonstrate this power (and skill) in front of both armies—to the glory of God!

In actuality, the fight wasn't much to write home about. If you had paid $49.95 on Pay-Per-View you would probably want your money back.

David didn't play by the rules of traditional combat. He was not about to play Goliath's game and get close enough for the big man to pick him up and tear him apart. David reached down, picked up five smooth stones, put them in his bag, and turned to face Goliath.

Then he took his staff in his hand, chose five smooth stones from the stream, put them in the pouch of his shepherd's bag and, with his sling in his hand, approached the Philistine.

(1 Samuel 17:40)

In his book *David and Goliath*, Malcolm Gladwell outlined how David approached Goliath, won the fight, and concluded it was over before it began!

Gladwell stated that ancient armies had three kinds of fighting men: first there was the calvary made up of armed men who rode on horseback or in chariots. Second came the infantry—foot soldiers wearing armor and carrying swords and shields (Goliath was an infantryman). The third was the artillery or projectile warriors—archers and, most importantly, slingers. David would be classified as a slinger.

Gladwell added:

> Slinging took an extraordinary amount of skill and practice. But in experienced hands, the sling was a devastating weapon. ...in the Old Testament book of Judges, slingers are described as being accurate within a "hair's breadth." [See Judges 20:16; 1 Chronicles 12:2.] An experienced slinger could kill or seriously injure a target at a distance of up to two hundred yards.

> ...Goliath is heavy infantry. He thinks that he is going to be engaged in a duel with another heavy-infantryman. ... When he says, "Come to me"...he means come right up to me so that we can fight at close quarters.

> ...David, however, has no intention of honoring the rituals of single combat. ...He *runs* toward Goliath, because without armor he has speed and maneuverability. He puts a rock into his sling, and whips it around and around, faster and faster at six or seven revolutions per second, aiming his projectile at Goliath's forehead—the giant's only point of vulnerability. Eitan Hirsch, a ballistics expert with the Israeli Defense Forces, recently did a series of calculations showing that a typical-size stone hurled by an expert

slinger at a distance of thirty-five meters would have hit Goliath's head with a velocity of thirty-four meters per second—more than enough to penetrate his skull and render him unconscious or dead. In terms of stopping power, that is equivalent to a fair-size modern handgun. "We find," Hirsch writes, "that David could have slung and hit Goliath in little more than one second—a time so brief that Goliath would not have been able to protect himself...."

"Goliath had as much chance against David," the historian Robert Dohrenwend writes, "as any Bronze Age warrior with a sword would have had against an [opponent] armed with a .45 automatic pistol."[4]

What Did David Gain?

I've heard it said that we should never take on a problem (a giant) that doesn't promise a reward on the other side. I don't know if David was thinking in those terms or not. I know he asked what would be done for the person who took down Goliath. Could it be that David realized that defeating Goliath would open the door for more advantages in the kingdom? I can't speak to his mental state; I can only go by what he said, what he did, and what he gained.

What did David gain? He was rewarded with the king's daughter, unlimited wealth, a covenant friend (Jonathan), and tax exemption for his entire family. From appearances, it seemed David was on the fast track to a huge promotion.

Goliath became a bridge from David's present to his future. Little did David know that Goliath was his doorway to promotion. Don't run from your promotion, even if a giant is standing in your way.

> God does not want our faith kept in mothballs, so He sometimes allows trials and testing to come into our lives; the unexpected hardships and heartbreaks that rock us in places we never thought we'd face as a child of God. And it's in those defining moments that we knock off the cobwebs of our everyday faith and face life with a new and improved one that's empowered by God Himself.
>
> —Ron Lambros[5]

WHAT CAN WE LEARN?

1. Remember Past Victories

David rehearsed to Saul how God came through for him in the past. We need to do the same. It becomes a source of strength to know that God did come through for us when we faced our last test. The problem is we don't celebrate enough of God's past victories. When faced with a new Goliath, sometimes the only thing that comes out in me is fear, not celebration. Stop remembering your defeats and start rehearsing your victories!

Remember those times when you didn't think you would make it—and you did? It becomes a source of courage to stand up to today's challenges to know that God did it in the past, and He will do it again today! Now you have the courage to go forward.

2. David's Victory Mobilized an Entire Army

Our victory can be a great inspiration to others who have been bound by fear. We can be a source of inspiration and a bondage breaker in the lives of others when we set the example by defeating the enemy. As a result, many others will rise in faith and accomplish great things for God.

Determine to become someone's inspiration to face their Goliath. Lead the way and show them *it can be done!*

3. Don't Tolerate Giants—Kill Them!

It's been said that we will never change what we tolerate. I would add that you will never kill a giant when you try to negotiate a compromise. Giants don't compromise or negotiate—they want to render you helpless and harmless.

As I stated earlier, at some point we, like Israel's army, will face a giant. Your giant may not be over nine feet tall, but trust me—when you're facing one, it may appear so massive that it blots out the Son!

Enemy after enemy confronts us as we walk throughout life. Sometimes these enemies are defiant and frightening, and we feel overpowered and overwhelmed. The enemies might include circumstances that create all kinds of trials: temptations, accidents, disease, financial difficulty, depression, discouragement, purposelessness, or the death of a loved one.

You may not think so, but like David there is a warrior inside each of us. Remember—we are on the winning side. *"The one who is in you is greater than the one who is in the world"* (1 John 4:4). As we become faithful in the smaller tests, we will see God come through—when we face our Goliath.

It's the little test that prepares us for something much greater. None of the obstacles that were thrown at David deterred him from becoming the greatest GGK in Israel's history. What God did for David, He will do for us!

Notes

1. Russell Johnston. AZQuotes.com, Wind and Fly LTD, 2022. https://www.azquotes.com/author/23737-Russell_Johnston. accessed June 5, 2022.

2. https://www.christianquotes.info/quotes-by-topic/quotes-about-trials/ accessed June 5, 2022.

3. Neal Maxwell, "It' Service, Not Status, That Counts," qtd. in Corey H. Maxwell, ed., *Neal A. Maxwell Quote Book* (Bookcraft Pubs, 2001).

4. Malcolm Gladwell, *David and Goliath* (New York, NY: Little, Brown and Co., 2013), 10-11.

5. Ron Lambros, *All My Love, Jesus: Personal Reminders From the Heart of God* (Bowker Identifier Services, 2019), 105.

Section II

WARRIORS
IN TESTING

5

FRIENDS AND ENEMIES

When a sinister person means to be your enemy, they always start by trying to become your friend.

—attributed to William Blake

After David had finished talking with Saul, Jonathan became one in spirit with David, and he loved him as himself. From that day Saul kept David with him and did not let him return home to his family. And Jonathan made a covenant with David because he loved him as himself. Jonathan took off the robe he was wearing and gave it to David, along with his tunic, and even his sword, his bow and his belt. Whatever mission Saul sent him on, David was so successful that Saul gave him a high rank in the army. This pleased all the troops, and Saul's officers as well.

—1 Samuel 18:1-5

INTRODUCTION

The moment David picked up the five smooth stones, his life changed forever. He would no longer be just a shepherd boy tending his father's flock. He performed his duties as a shepherd by killing a lion and a bear; and at the end of the day, he took down a giant and saved the nation from destruction.

He is now David—GGK (Great Giant Killer)!

Not only did he become a hero to the nation, but he also received a new covenant friend, Jonathan; a beautiful wife, Michal; and a position of authority in the king's court, commander of the army.

David must have thought, *I've got it made; I'm on top of the world.* But he didn't consider his success a breeding ground for trouble. It's a fact in the natural and spiritual that any level of success will bring on opposition.

When facing trouble, some people fold up, some people crack up, some people face up to the challenge. Author Catherine Pulsifer wrote an excellent article entitled "Three Kinds of Trouble." In her article, she outlined a sound strategy that will keep us moving forward during life's troubles. She wrote:

> Since trouble can be found around any corner, you must decide now how you will handle trouble. If you decide to just sit and complain, you will stay stuck in the same place; if you decide that you will turn trouble into a valued learning experience, and an experience that can help you through future difficulties, then you are on the right

path. Part of the arsenal to handle future issues is the development of a sound strategy that can help you overcome almost any circumstance.[1]

I agree with Pulsifer's analysis. While trouble can be found around every corner, it's always best to strategize a way to make "trouble" work for you and not against you.

Friends and Enemies

If David thought that Goliath was his most significant test of faith and courage, he would soon find out that serving Saul would present challenges that he never considered. New challenges came at him from all sides; friends and enemies were waiting for him just around the corner!

David and Jonathan: The Test of Friendship

As soon as Jonathan heard David speak, something happened that changed the relationship. *"After David had finished talking with Saul, Jonathan became one in spirit with David, and he loved him as himself"* (1 Samuel 18:1-2). Jonathan was the king's son and a man of faith, courage, vision, and unselfishness in his own right. He saw something in David that touched his heart, which moved him to make a covenant with David.

And Jonathan made a covenant with David because he loved him as himself. Jonathan took off the robe he was wearing and gave it to David, along with his tunic, and even his sword, his bow and his belt.

(1 Samuel 18:3-4)

We didn't find any jealousy between the two men as the relationship progressed. It would have been easy for Jonathan to harbor resentment toward David; after all, he (Jonathan) was the king's son, next in line to take the throne of his father. Jonathan had enough spiritual insight to understand that David, not himself, would be next in line to sit on the throne.

The relationship between these two men was no ordinary friendship. No doubt David had many people around him that wanted to be his friend, but the bond between David and Jonathan was at another level. C.S. Lewis explained that true friends *face in the same direction* toward common projects, interests, and goals. From all appearances, David and Jonathan had the kind of relationship Lewis described.

Five Ingredients of a True Friend

1. Trustworthy

Trust is the "glue" that holds covenant relationships together. It may take years to build that level of trust (seen between David and Jonathan), but it can only take a few minutes of indiscretion to break it apart. Without trust, there can never be an open and honest friendship. Proverbs 18:24 tells us, *"One who has unreliable friends soon comes to ruin, but there is a friend who sticks closer than a brother."*

2. Protective

Jonathan was willing to put his life on the line for David on more than one occasion. Jonathan kept David safe even though he had to go against his father, the king. Sacrificing oneself for a friend is not something that a casual acquaintance does—it's much more profound and more potent than that. John 15:13 best describes the attitude of Jonathan toward David: *"Greater love has no one than this: to lay down one's life for one's friends."*

3. No Hidden Agenda

If Jonathan had a hidden agenda to get rid of David, he had a funny way of showing it. When the occasion presented itself to be negative toward David, Jonathan did the opposite—he defended him to his father. First Samuel 19:4-5 says:

> *Jonathan spoke well of David to Saul his father and said to him, "Let not the king do wrong to his servant David; he has not wronged you, and what he has done has benefited you greatly. He took his life in his hands when he killed the Philistine. The Lord won a great victory for all Israel, and you saw it and were glad. Why then would you do wrong to an innocent man like David by killing him for no reason?"*

4. It Will Allow You to Be Real

A true friend will allow you to be yourself, even when you stumble and fall. It has been said that in one's lifetime, we may have only one or two true friends who know us, warts and all, and will stick by us through all of life's ups and downs. I love this quote of Henry Ward Beecher, who said,: "Every man should keep a fair-sized cemetery in which to bury the faults of his friends."[2]

5. Encouraging

One of the most beautiful pictures of true friendship is how Jonathan encouraged David when he was on the run from Saul:

> *While David was at Horesh in the Desert of Ziph, he learned that Saul had come out to take his life. And Saul's son Jonathan went to David at Horesh and helped him find strength in God.*
>
> (1 Samuel 23:15-16)

David and Saul: The Test of Authority

The relationship between David and Saul was complicated. David learned that taking down Goliath and becoming the most famous giant killer in the land had its pitfalls.

David did nothing to justify Saul's treatment of him. David recognized that Saul was still in a position of authority over him in all his actions and attitudes. As time progressed and Saul became more irrational, it would have been easy for David to conclude it was a wasted effort trying to please the king. He could have said, "Why should I try when everything I do is wrong!"

No matter what we do, there will always be people around us who are difficult to handle. On the one hand, there was Jonathan, who made a covenant with David and gave him his loyalty and friendship; on the other hand, Saul's anger was so "hot" against David that it eventually drove David out of the king's palace into the wilderness.

What prompted Saul's anger toward David?

Jealousy

When Saul and his army came home, 1 Samuel 18:6-9 tells us:

> *When the men were returning home after David had killed the Philistine, the women came out from all the towns of Israel to meet King Saul with singing and dancing, with joyful songs and with timbrels and lyres. As they danced, they sang: "Saul has slain his thousands, and David his tens of thousands." Saul was very angry; this refrain displeased him greatly. "They have credited David with tens of thousands," he thought, "but me with only thousands. What more can he get but the kingdom?" And from that time on Saul kept a close eye on David.*

Saul was so jealous of David that the next day while David was playing the harp, Saul threw a spear at him, but fortunately David ducked! Why would Saul do such a thing? He did it because of what others were saying about David. It wasn't David bragging about himself; it was what other people were saying about him. He had no control over that, but it didn't matter to Saul. He allowed his anger and jealousy to rob him of any spiritual judgment.

> *The next day an evil spirit from God came forcefully on Saul. He was prophesying in his house, while David was playing the lyre, as he usually did. Saul had a spear in his hand and he hurled it, saying to himself, "I'll pin David to the wall." But David eluded him twice. Saul was afraid of David, because the Lord was with David but had departed from Saul.*
>
> (1 Samuel 18:10-12)

If you are under attack, understand that God has a blessing scheduled in your life. You face trials and attacks because satan will always attack the next person in line who is due a promotion. I believe satan knows what's coming, so his goal is to discourage you and get you so depressed that you will walk away and give up. If you give in to the enemy, you will miss out on all God has promised to fulfill in your life.

Jesus told His disciples with great rewards for sacrifice and great blessings come persecutions:

> *Then Peter spoke up, "We have left everything to follow you!" "Truly I tell you," Jesus replied, "no one who has left home or brothers or sisters or mother or father or children or fields for me and the gospel will fail to receive a hundred times as much in this present age: homes, brothers, sisters, mothers, children and fields—along with persecutions—and in the age to come eternal life."*
>
> (Mark 10:28-30)

Having success doesn't mean you are exempt from problems or trials. The more success you have, the more problems you will face. There will always be those around you who don't understand where promotion, blessing, and favor originate. Spiritual success does not come from luck, fate, or being in the right place at the right time. It's not a matter of "knowing the right people."

Spiritual success is *received* not *achieved*. David put it this way:

> *"Do not lift your horns against heaven; do not speak so defiantly." No one from the east or the west or from the desert can exalt themselves. It is God who judges: he brings one down, he exalts another.*
>
> (Psalm 75:5-7)

David was not successful because he bragged about himself. He didn't receive the anointing to be king because he was in the right place at the right time. He was not a self-promoter who wormed his way into certain friendships with cunning manipulation. David was not looking for a promotion. He was just a faithful servant satisfied with obeying his father and tending sheep.

No doubt, many men in the kingdom were stronger, wiser, and would have made better military leaders. How many of those guys would have loved to be in David's shoes? But God didn't choose them; He chose David. Why? God saw that David would be faithful and rewarded him with a fresh anointing to be king.

Now watch. I want you to see that jealousy and envy breed another powerful emotion.

Insecurity

David just continued to do what he was supposed to do, leading the troops of Israel in battle. In everything he did, he achieved great success, making Saul even more afraid of him.

> *So he sent David away from him and gave him command over a thousand men, and David led the troops in their campaigns. In everything he did he had great success, because the Lord was with him. When Saul saw how successful he was, he was afraid of him.*
>
> (1 Samuel 18:13-15)

Remember, Saul had offered to give his daughter to the man who killed Goliath, and now he was going to fulfill his promise. But do you think Saul kept his original promise? No, absolutely not! The daughter who was promised was given to another man. *"So when the time came for Merab, Saul's daughter, to be given to David, she was given in marriage to Adriel of Meholah"* (1 Samuel 18:19).

Then Saul came up with another idea. He would use his youngest daughter, Michal, as a way to have David killed. He demanded what seemed to be an impossible task from David: "kill me one hundred Philistines!" I'm sure Saul thought it was a foolproof plan. He would send David out against the Philistines, and the enemy would kill David. There was only one problem. The Lord was with David, killing not one hundred but two hundred of the Philistines! Saul had no choice but to give David his daughter in marriage.

Think about that evilness of Saul's heart. He was willing to use his daughter as a pawn in a personal vendetta. When people get to this point with envy, strife, and jealousy, they become blind to the good things. Everything they see is viewed through the lens of their bitterness. When Saul finally realized that the Lord was with David, and how much Michal loved him, it caused Saul to become more afraid. *"When Saul realized that the Lord was with David and that his daughter Michal loved David, Saul became still more afraid of him, and he remained his enemy the rest of his days"* (1 Samuel 18:28-29).

Dealing with a difficult man did not stop David from doing what God had called him to do. He continued to defeat the enemies of Israel and became a national hero. Everyone in the palace knew of Saul's plan to kill David. *"Saul told his son Jonathan and all the attendants to kill David. But Jonathan had taken a great liking to David"* (1 Samuel 19:1).

What does all this tell us? When blessings and favor come our way, we better prepare for a fight. Warriors are constantly tested, and David was no exception!

WHAT CAN WE LEARN?

1. Everyone Has Enemies

When David was just a humble shepherd boy playing his harp for the king, everything was rosy, but as soon as David achieved success, he went from being Saul's favorite to Saul's enemy. Believe it or not, David's number-one enemy was not Goliath or the army of the Philistines. No, his number-one enemy was the guy sitting on the throne who had lost his anointing.

Nothing is more dangerous in the Kingdom of God than someone who has lost the anointing but still has a measure of authority. Trust me, they will do everything to maintain their turf, even if it means eliminating a "David" who walks in a greater anointing!

2. Enemies Have a Purpose

David had enemies, Jesus had enemies, and I have enemies. Don't worry: if you do anything for the Kingdom of God, you too, will have enemies! As one teacher said, "If what we're doing does not draw opposition from the enemy, we must check and see what we're doing." I can guarantee you when the enemy attacks, you will quickly find out who your friends are!

> You have enemies? Good. That means you've stood up for something, sometime in your life."
>
> —Winston Churchill

3. Everyone Needs the Encouragement of a Friend

One of the byproducts of dealing with enemies is discouragement, and no one is immune, not even some of the greatest prophets.

Remember the prophet Elijah? After his mountaintop victory he ran from Jezebel, fearing for his life. He found himself in the pit of despair, all alone with nowhere to go—and no friends in sight. He ended up under a juniper tree (nothing more than a desert scrub brush) and wanted to die. He was tired, depressed, and most of all filled with fear. How did the Lord treat him? Did He send an angel to confront him about his condition? Did the Lord boom from Heaven and tell Elijah that prophets don't act this way? *No!* The Lord sent an angel to comfort, feed, and encourage him. The Lord knew for Elijah to carry on his mission, he had to regain his strength. He didn't need a sermon—he needed a true friend who would help him in a time of need (see 1 Kings 19:1-8).

Keep in mind that even earthly friendships may have their moments when things go south. No relationship is perfect—even Jonathan and David's relationship presented its challenges. But there is one true friend that will never fail or disappoint. Jesus called His followers friends.

> *I no longer call you servants, because a servant does not know his master's business. Instead, I have called you friends, for everything that I learned from my Father I have made known to you.*
>
> (John 15:15)

Warren Wiersbe writes:

> He calls us friends and not slaves; no master stoops to explain his plans to a slave; but a friend shares his heart and mind with those who are dear to him. The word Jesus uses for "friends" is used in Greek literature for "an intimate at court." We are friends of the King! He wants to share himself and his plans with us.[3]

NOTES

1. Catherine Pulsifer, Three Kinds of Trouble, https://www.wow4u
   .com/threetroubles/ accessed June 23, 2022.

2. Chaplain W.L. Roset, contributor, *Live*, Assemblies of God USA,
   March 23, 1980, page 16, https://pentecostalarchives
   .org/?a=d&d=LIVE198003-01.1.16.

3. Warren W. Wiersbe, *5 Secrets of Living* (Wheaton, IL: Tyndale
   House, 1977), 76.

6

LESSONS FROM THE CAVE

That cave was no longer David's escape hatch. If you can believe it, the smelly, dank cave became a place of training for those who were the beginning of the army that would be called "David's mighty men of valor."

—Charles R. Swindoll[1]

David left Gath and escaped to the cave of Adullam. When his brothers and his father's household heard about it, they went down to him there. All those who were in distress or in debt or discontented gathered around him, and he became their commander. About four hundred men were with him.

—1 Samuel 22:1-2

INTRODUCTION

One would think that ending up in a dark, damp, smelly cave at Adullam would not be the ideal place to receive another level of training. Here sat the future king of Israel hiding in a cave, hoping that his time to ascend the throne would come sooner rather than later.

It would be easy to look at David's experience in the cave as punishment instead of viewing the cave as another level of his development. David's success did not exempt him from the jealousy and fear of others, most notably King Saul.

David knew the taste of victory and the sweet smell of success at a young age (see 1 Samuel 17–20). He must have felt invincible after taking down Goliath and becoming a part of the inner circle in the king's court. But as the early morning mist burned away with the sun's rising, his standing with Saul went from hero to zero in the blink of an eye.

We often misinterpret our initial success as a never-ending journey that will take us from one level of success to another without difficulties or problems. Nothing could be further from the truth! Alan Redpath observed:

> So often the Providence of God seemed to run completely counter to His promises, but only that He may test our faith, only that He may ultimately accomplish his purpose for our lives in a way he could never do if the path were always smooth. It is when problems and difficulties seem to be overwhelming that the man of God learns some lessons that he could never learn otherwise. It isn't easy to walk with God, for the air at that height is somewhat rare. It is pure but sometimes it is hard to breathe, and faith almost gives up in the attempt to keep pace with God's way with His child.[2]

As the old saying goes, "Success does not insulate you from problems; it brings them on!"

———•◆•———

Three Important Lessons for Cave Dwellers

1. Don't Go by What You See

It's easy to misinterpret adverse circumstances. So often, we view whatever "bad thing" is happening at the moment as a death sentence to our dreams. David may have felt that way as he made his way to Adullam's cave. David quickly learned that it's better to go by what God says about you rather than by what you see around you!

When we read about David's journey to the cave, we have to ask, "What's a nice guy like you doing in a place like this?" Seriously, how did this young anointed warrior end up hiding in a cave?

It didn't happen by accident. There were circumstances (none of them good) that led David to such an uninviting place. At first glance, hiding in a cave would suggest that Samuel was wrong to anoint David king. Did Samuel make a mistake and anoint the wrong guy? Remember what the Lord told Samuel in 1 Samuel 16:7:

> *But the Lord said to Samuel, "Do not consider his appearance or his height, for I have rejected him. The Lord does not look at the things people look at. People look at the outward appearance, but the Lord looks at the heart."*

The answer is absolutely not! Samuel didn't make a mistake. David was the guy God chose—end of the story. But that didn't mean there wouldn't be challenges.

The road to the throne was filled with potholes, detours, and training venues. The *How to Be a King for Dummies* handbook listed none of these!

As one might expect, he stumbled along the way and faltered in his faith. He was young and successful, but he displayed poor judgment when confronted with issues he didn't know how to handle. David is not the first (and won't be the last) leader to make a wrong decision when faced with pressure.

First Samuel 21–22 show that instead of trusting in God, David trusted his instincts. He faltered in his faith, which sent him on the run.

The road to Adullam's cave was paved with fear and lies.

He conspired to lie to Saul (1 Samuel 20:1-42).

In his conversation with Jonathan, David displayed impatience and self-centeredness. *"Then David fled from Naioth at Ramah and went to Jonathan and asked, 'What have I done? What is my crime? How have I wronged your father, that he is trying to kill me?'"* (1 Samuel 20:1).

Obviously, if David and Jonathan had spent more time praying and less time scheming, the lies might not have been necessary. To help David, Jonathan ended up lying to his father about David's location. The entirety of 1 Samuel 20 is one lie after the other. Saul gave himself to wickedness, but that was no excuse for David to trust more in Jonathan's word than waiting to hear from God! C.S. Lewis once remarked, "A little lie is like a little pregnancy—it doesn't take long before everyone knows." That was certainly the case with David. What started as one "little" lie became a massive problem down the road!

He lied to Ahimelech (1 Samuel 21:1-9).

At this point, Scripture does not paint a pretty picture of David. After his farewell to Jonathan, David went to Nob, a small city about two miles north of Jerusalem, instead of waiting to hear the Lord's direction. Nob was the location of the Tabernacle in the wilderness. Who knows why David went there? Maybe it was to visit the Tabernacle once more before fleeing for his life. Or perhaps he was simply there to seek help from Ahimelech, the high priest (the grandson of Eli).

Ahimelech was suspicious and frightened at the arrival of Israel's most famous warrior. David arrived without an escort, which was very unusual, and caused the high priest to be more fearful of David.

> *David went to Nob, to Ahimelek the priest. Ahimelek trembled when he met him, and asked, "Why are you alone? Why is no one with you?"*
>
> (1 Samuel 21:1)

Instead of telling Ahimelech the truth, as David should have, what did this man "after God's own heart" do? He lied and said that Saul had sent him on a secret mission.

*David answered Ahimelek the priest, "The king sent me on
a mission and said to me, 'No one is to know anything about
the mission I am sending you on.' As for my men, I have told
them to meet me at a certain place. Now then, what do you
have on hand? Give me five loaves of bread, or whatever you
can find."*

(1 Samuel 21:2-3)

At first glance, it seems like a harmless lie. But this little white lie would lead to one of the most horrible massacres in the entire Word of God.

David asked Ahimelech for something to eat. The priest told him there was nothing to eat except the Bread of Presence. This was holy bread and was to be eaten only by the priest. This bread was a symbol of God's physical care for His people. I am convinced this being the only bread to eat was no accident. God was about the ambush David; all of this was a setup.

God reminded David of His promise to take care of his needs and the needs of the people. David was blinded by fear, so he could not see what was right in front of his eyes. When you are walking in fear and falter in your faith, you will be blinded to God's provision!

David was not only hungry, he was unarmed and fearful. He asked Ahimelech for a spear and a sword.

*The priest replied, "The sword of Goliath the Philistine,
whom you killed in the Valley of Elah, is here; it is wrapped
in a cloth behind the ephod. If you want it, take it; there is*

no sword here but that one." David said, "There is none like
it; give it to me."

(1 Samuel 21:9)

The high priest offered David the only available weapon. It was a war
trophy to remind the Israelites of God's protection.

The minute David picked up the sword, it should have reminded
him of God's faithfulness and power. Four or five years earlier, he had
defeated the man who carried that sword with nothing more than a
rock. But David's fear of Saul and his fear of his enemy caused him to
forget what he should do when faced with a giant problem. David failed
to remember the victories God gave him and instead continued to lean
on his own strength.

At this point, David's plan seemed successful. However, one of Saul's
spies, a man by the name of Doeg, recognized David (see 1 Samuel
21:7). He saw and heard everything that went on, ultimately leading to
a horrible massacre (see 1 Samuel 22:16-19).

He lied to Achish (1 Samuel 21:10-15).

David's situation went from bad to worse, as it always does when we trust
in ourselves and our wisdom rather than trusting the wisdom of God.
Proverbs 29:25 says, *"Fear of man will prove to be a snare, but whoever trusts
in the Lord is kept safe."* What started as one lie became two, and before
David realized what was happening, his life was spiraling out of control.

Having been exposed, what did David do? Rather than telling the
truth and trusting God, he ran to Gath. Gath was enemy territory and

the hometown of Goliath. Undoubtedly, David thought this would probably be the last place Saul would look for him. But again, David was recognized (see 1 Samuel 21:11-12). And so David sank to a new low, pretending to be insane. While in their presence, he acted like a madman. He made marks on the door of the gate and let drool run down his beard (see 1 Samuel 21:13). The anointed king of Israel, the greatest hero the nation had ever known, acted like a fool, but his deception worked. The Lord intervened and turned the king's heart away from getting rid of David.

Sometimes when we look at our adverse circumstances, we think God's plan for our life has been derailed, but it will only be derailed if we allow it to be. David knew that God had a plan for his life. Despite his faltering faith, he kept moving forward until what God said about his future was more important than the circumstances he saw before his eyes.

2. Anchor Your Hope in God—Not Other People

In Adullam's cave, David learned that he was without hope unless his life was anchored in God. Little by little, everyone and everything that David leaned on was being removed. Instead of reigning, David was running. At this point, David's life could be summed up with one word—*lost!*

He lost his promotion.

One of the "perks" of defeating Goliath was a high position in Saul's army. It was suggested that David become the head of Saul's bodyguard (see 1 Samuel 18:12-16), but because of Saul's jealousy he was demoted to a low-ranking captain of over a thousand men. David maintained his humility despite his demotion, but it had to hurt when he knew he had done nothing wrong.

He lost his wife.

Another "perk" of defeating Goliath was the promise of the king's daughter. But that daughter was given to another man; Saul again refused to keep his word. David would be given Michal as a "consolation prize." Saul used Michal as a tool to have David killed. The king demanded an impossible dowry, hoping David would die in battle, but the Lord gave him the victory and the mission was successful (see 1 Samuel 18:17-30). The marriage to Michal was not happy, and while David was on the run he lost her to another man (see 1 Samuel 25:44).

He lost the prophet.

Not surprisingly, David sought out Samuel, the prophet who had anointed him king. But before David could benefit from Samuel's wise counsel, Saul found out David's location. Once again, David was on the run. No longer could he depend on the prophet for direction.

> When David had fled and made his escape, he went to Samuel at Ramah and told him all that Saul had done to him. Then he and Samuel went to Naioth and stayed there. Word came to Saul: "David is in Naioth at Ramah."
>
> (1 Samuel 19:18-19)

He lost his best friend.

After realizing that Samuel could no longer help him, he ran to his best friend, Jonathan. *"Then David fled from Naioth at Ramah and went to Jonathan and asked, 'What have I done? What is my crime? How have I wronged your father, that he is trying to kill me?'"* (1 Samuel 20:1). In the exchange between the two men, it becomes apparent that David thought his death was just a matter of time. While David was on the run avoiding Saul, Jonathan returned to his father's house (see 1 Samuel 20:42).

He lost his self-respect.

As we discussed earlier, David pretended to be insane—in Gath, of all places! After acting crazy in Gath, he escaped to the cave of Adullam. This lonely cave was about twelve miles southwest of Jerusalem. He was separated from Saul's court and considered a rebel and an outlaw.

It was in the cave where David began to reflect on his life. He was discovering what it was like to have everyone he cared about betray him. Being treated like a fugitive and hunted down like a rabid dog is not listed in the handbook either! But the cave experience would not be lost on David. It was in the cave that David would learn how to anchor himself in the Lord!

3. The Cave Experience Is a Training Ground

"David left Gath and escaped to the cave of Adullam" (1 Samuel 22:1). During the cave experience, David wrote at least three psalms to express

his feelings. These three psalms (34, 57, and 142) give us a glimpse into David's heart. He was alone, (briefly) afraid, and filled with despair.

These psalms were written to show his spiritual revival as he reflected on the fact that he now must trust God and God alone. One can feel David's despair in a few short verses:

> *Look and see, there is no one at my right hand; no one is concerned for me. I have no refuge; no one cares for my life. I cry to you, Lord; I say, "You are my refuge, my portion in the land of the living." Listen to my cry, for I am in desperate need; rescue me from those who pursue me, for they are too strong for me.*
>
> (Psalm 142:4-6)

But David was not alone for long. David's family, along with a strange lot of about four hundred men, joined him in the cave: *"David left Gath and escaped to the cave of Adullam. When his brothers and his father's household heard about it, they went down to him there"* (1 Samuel 22:1).

I would have no idea if David was surprised to see his family crowd into the cave with him or not. But there they were. Yes, this is the family that all but relegated David to the "oh, by the way, there is one more son" page in the family scrapbook (see 1 Samuel 16:11-12). Yet God knew that David needed companionship from those who knew him best.

But suddenly, another group of folks showed up at the cave. And what a group it was! They are described this way: *"All those who were in distress or in debt or discontented gathered around him, and he became their commander. About four hundred men were with him"* (1 Samuel 22:2)

Let's face it, David was not building the fastest-growing church in town. If this church had a name, it would have been called "The First Fellowship of the Depressed, Stressed, Debtors, and Discouraged."

If David thought he would have some "alone time" to pray and gather his thoughts, he misunderstood what God was doing. David was learning how to minister to those in need, all while having his own needs. I can almost see David sitting around the campfire, teaching and instructing this motley crew about learning to trust God in the dark times. Maybe he spoke in the words of Psalm 34:11: *"Come, my children, listen to me; I will teach you the fear of the Lord."*

Something happened to David in that cave. He learned in the wilderness to trust God, not men. David remembered God's promises and began to show his leadership ability. He turned this motley crew into one of Israel's greatest armies. Eventually they would grow into an army of six hundred and become famous as David's mighty men (see 1 Samuel 23:13; 1 Chronicles 12:8)!

———•◆•———

WHAT CAN WE LEARN?

1. You're Never Alone (Even in the Cave)

One of the worst feelings in the world is the thought that we have been abandoned by everyone. When trust is broken, we may feel that all hope is gone. As David sat by the flickering fire and pondered his life, he looked up to heaven and declared:

> *Have mercy on me, my God, have mercy on me, for in you I take refuge. I will take refuge in the shadow of your wings until the disaster has passed. I cry out to God Most High, to God, who vindicates me. He sends from heaven and saves me, rebuking those who hotly pursue me—God sends forth his love and his faithfulness.*
>
> (Psalm 57:1-3)

We must discover, as David did, that when we anchor our hope in others, they will fail us sooner or later—but God never will! Heather Riggleman said:

> Yet we have a promise from God that He will never leave us or forsake us. God is at work in us, in our difficulties, and in situations even though trials and challenges will not always be removed from our lives.
>
> Hebrews 13:5 is our promise and foundation of the love God has for us. "I will never leave you nor forsake you."

In a world constantly changing because of the people, finances, and things around us, God's promise to never leave us is encouraging.[3]

2. Leadership Development Will Often Take Place in Unusual Places

I doubt many of us would choose a dark, smelly cave to hone our leadership skills. But here we are with David and a motley bunch of men who were not considered the best of the best. At one point, these men were in debt, discontented, and distressed, with nowhere else to turn. They decided to cast their lot in with another who was in the same boat.

David decided he was going to make the best of a bad situation. I can picture David looking around and saying, "If we are going to be stuck together in a cave, we might as well do some training."

Most of the time, we don't pick the classrooms to learn leadership skills. Signing up for a weekend seminar on "Ten Easy Lessons on How to Lead" is not the kind of leadership training that will enable you to take a bunch of malcontents and shape them into a mighty fighting force (see 1 Chronicles 12:1-18).

3. The Cave Experiences Are Temporary

There's an old adage that says, "It came to pass; it didn't come to stay." During times of adversity, we often feel as if whatever we are going through is a permanent situation, but it's not. It's only temporary.

David's cave experience ended, but we will see it was not the end of his training. Fourteen years passed from the time of his initial anointing by Samuel until he took the throne of a united Israel. Each phase of his training was another step toward the ultimate goal—the throne.

The lesson for David (and us) is to trust God that He knows best how to take us from where we are to where we are going!

NOTES

1. Charles R. Swindoll, *David: A Man of Passion and Destiny*, 123.

2. Alan Redpath, *The Making of a Man of God* (Grand Rapids, MI: Fleming H. Revell, 2004), 82.

3. Heather Riggleman, "Will God Never Leave Us Nor Forsake Us?" Christianity.com, February 19, 2021, https://www.christianity.com/wiki/god/will-god-never-leave-us-nor-forsake-us.html.

7

HOW TO SPEAK TO AN ANGRY MAN

If you speak when angry, you'll make the best speech you'll ever regret.

—Groucho Marx[1]

When Abigail saw David, she quickly got off her donkey and bowed down before David with her face to the ground. She fell at his feet and said: "Pardon your servant, my lord, and let me speak to you; hear what your servant has to say. Please pay no attention, my lord, to that wicked man Nabal. He is just like his name—his name means Fool, and folly goes with him. And as for me, your servant, I did not see the men my lord sent. And now, my lord, as surely as the Lord your God lives and as you live, since the Lord has kept you from bloodshed and from avenging yourself with your own hands, may your enemies and all who are intent on harming my lord be like Nabal. And let this gift, which your servant has brought to my lord, be given to the men who follow you.

—1 Samuel 25:23-27

INTRODUCTION

The last time we saw David, he was hiding in a cave surrounded by his family and a few hundred of his new best friends (see 1 Samuel 22:1-2). If David thought his cave experience was the last of his "training for reigning," he was sadly mistaken. David was caught between two worlds—*the world of promise* and *the world of reality*. The promise said, "You are the anointed king, and you will sit on the throne." But his reality was quite different from the promise. David was learning that a process takes you from the promise to the fulfillment of God's Word.

So far, his kingdom consisted of a few hundred malcontents. And to top it off, the current king was hunting him—not to congratulate him, but to hang him up by his thumbs until he died! I doubt it was the kind of life he envisioned when Samuel doused his head in oil.

A significant part of David's training involved self-control. If he was ever going to reign over a united Israel and rule with the heart of God, he must learn how to control himself, especially his emotions. What better way to learn than to be placed in a situation in which he would have to choose? On the one hand, he could allow his anger to control him; on the other hand, he could listen to wise counsel and pull back from the brink of disaster.

A DRAMA IN FOUR PARTS

Let's take a journey through 1 Samuel 25 and follow the drama as it unfolds. If this were a soap opera, millions would tune in to see how it would play out!

Part One: Samuel Is Dead

As 1 Samuel 25 opens, David is faced with another gut punch. Samuel, his mentor, friend, and confidant, is dead. *"Now Samuel died, and all Israel assembled and mourned for him; and they buried him at his home in Ramah. Then David moved down into the Desert of Paran"* (1 Samuel 25:1).

Samuel was the prophet, priest, and judge of Israel. He served God faithfully, even at the risk of his own life. No doubt, had King Saul known that he had anointed David as the new king of Israel, he would have killed him. Saul would have viewed Samuel's actions as the ultimate betrayal.

There is also little doubt that Samuel's death caused a whirlwind of emotions in David. Samuel was the man of God in David's life, a trusted ally, and a spiritual mentor. David may have thought, *What will I do now that my anchor is gone?* David suddenly became a ship drifting on the open sea without a rudder, and *as we shall soon see, it showed in his dealings with Nabal.*

Probably one of the most difficult times in my life and yours is when the "Samuels" pass on, and we are left with a gigantic hole to fill. It is a tough thing to overcome. Whether we want to admit it or not, there are times when God will remove certain people from our life to get our attention. Yes, it can be upsetting and confusing, and if we are not careful we will miss what God is trying to teach us.

For instance, Isaiah said, *"In the year that King Uzziah died, I saw the Lord, high and exalted, seated on a throne; and the train of his robe filled the temple"* (Isaiah 6:1). What was Isaiah saying in his declaration? As you study the rest of the chapter, it is evident that only when the king was removed could he (Isaiah) see God more clearly. That was God's plan for Isaiah—and David.

I have been there, and maybe you have too. When a person we look up to is removed from our life, we have a choice. We can blame God for taking them or rejoice in their contribution to our life. We always have a choice when tough times come.

Instead of getting closer to God, David went in the other direction. The death of Samuel knocked him off balance. Instead of seeing God more clearly, he became filled with depression and discouragement. While David was still reeling over the loss of Samuel, he found himself with an unexpected challenge.

Part Two: Nabal the Fool

Nabal's name means "foolish or wicked." One has to wonder if his mother understood what she was doing when she pinned that name on him. Whatever the reason, it was not far off from his character. Everything about him screamed, "Fool!"

A certain man in Maon, who had property there at Carmel, was very wealthy. He had a thousand goats and three *thousand sheep, which he was shearing in Carmel. His name was Nabal and his wife's name was Abigail. She was an intelligent and beautiful woman, **but her husband was surly and mean** in his dealings—he was a Calebite.*

(1 Samuel 25:2-3)

Charles Swindoll said:

Understand, that didn't mean a person was simple minded. In the scriptures a fool was a person who said, "There is no God!" He lived his life as though there were no God. Furthermore, we are told that "the man was harsh" (25:3). The Hebrew word here means "hard, stubborn, belligerent." Furthermore, it says he was "evil in his dealings" (25:3). That means he was dishonest. Quite a combination! Nabal was demanding, deceptive, and unfair.[2]

We are also told that Nabal was very wealthy. He had three thousand sheep and a thousand goats; to all appearances, he was one of the richest men in the region. In our day, you might say he was loaded or "flushed with cash." Nabal was not the first and won't be the last to think that an abundance of possessions gave him the right to have unlimited power over others.

David sent some of his men to Nabal to ask for food. David's request was reasonable because he and his men had protected Nabal's flocks for a considerable time. David had to assume that Nabal would readily give him food out of gratitude. Why wouldn't Nabal fulfill his request since David and his men had taken on protecting this man's property? After all, it was the accepted custom that when the sheep were sheared, the owner would share some of the profits with those willing to protect the shepherds while they were in the field. It was not extortion on David's part, nor a mafia-type protection racket. It was just standard practice.

> *While David was in the wilderness, he heard that Nabal was shearing sheep. So he sent ten young men and said to them, "Go up to Nabal at Carmel and greet him in my name. Say to him: 'Long life to you! Good health to you and your household! And good health to all that is yours!*
>
> *"'Now I hear that it is sheep-shearing time. When your shepherds were with us, we did not mistreat them, and the whole time they were at Carmel nothing of theirs was missing. Ask your own servants and they will tell you. Therefore be favorable toward my men, since we come at a festive time. Please give your servants and your son David whatever you can find for them."*
>
> (1 Samuel 25:4-8)

Instead of sending provisions, Nabal responded to David's request by hurling insults (see 1 Samuel 25:10). He was not about to share any of his leftovers with a bunch of fugitives.

It would be an understatement to say that Nabal made a serious miscalculation. For some strange reason, Nabal overestimated his power and influence and underestimated David's reaction. When dealing with the future king of Israel (David), it's not wise to refuse his request with a belligerent attitude, but Nabal did just that. He answered the requests of David's servants in the true greedy and surly spirit of Nabal:

> *Who is this David? Who is this son of Jesse? Many servants are breaking away from their masters these days. Why should I take my bread and water, and the meat I have slaughtered for my shearers, and give it to men coming from who knows where?*
>
> (1 Samuel 25:10-11)

Part Three: David Is Vengeful

What to do with a man who refused a simple request? David did not respond to Nabal in a "positive" manner. David sought revenge by sending his men to kill Nabal and all of his shepherds (see 1 Samuel 25:13).

As stated earlier, David and his six hundred fighting men had been moving about behind the scenes, fighting various wild tribes in the wilderness. In the process, they often protected shepherds from the attacks of these wild tribes. The wilderness of those days was dangerous, what you might call a high-crime district. Bandits frequented the area preying on travelers and plundering the defenseless.

In his book *The Making of a Man of God,* Alan Redpath made an interesting observation concerning David's response to Nabal:

> "I am justified in doing this," David would reply. "There is no reason why Nabal should treat me as he has. He has repaid all my kindness with insults. I will show him he

can't trifle with me. It is one thing to take it from Saul who is my superior at this point, but this sort of man—this high handed individual must be taught a lesson!"[3]

To say David was angry enough to kill might be an understatement—he wasn't just mad, he was filled with rage: "I want to kill you, your family, your shepherds, and even your pets!" David's anger was about to send him across a line from which there was no return.

David said to his men, "Each of you strap on your sword!" So they did, and David strapped his on as well. About four hundred men went up with David, while two hundred stayed with the supplies.

(1 Samuel 25:13)

As one Bible teacher observed:

It was bad enough that Saul should pursue David's life. But it was like pouring salt into a wound for David to also have to face contempt and harsh treatment from those of his own tribesmen who should have been loyal to him and who, as in the case of Nabal and the Keilahites, especially owed much of what they had to his valiant performances against the enemies of Israel. But David learned well what all God's people have to learn sooner or later; namely, this world does not do well in duly rewarding faithful service.[4]

Have you ever felt that way? So angry that you were ready to throw caution to the wind and allow your emotions to take control? Too bad

David didn't have his future son's reflections on the dangers of uncontrolled anger—his name was Solomon, and his reflections are called the *Proverbs.*

Solomon, who was never lost for words, explains that it is just as essential to keep our anger in check as it is to control our lust and our speech.

Just a brief sampling:

Whoever is patient has great understanding, but one who is quick-tempered displays folly.

(Proverbs 14:29)

A gentle answer turns away wrath, but a harsh word stirs up anger.

(Proverbs 15:1)

Better a patient person than a warrior, one with self-control, than one who takes a city.

(Proverbs 16:32)

A person's wisdom yields patience; it is to one's glory to over-look an offense.

(Proverbs 19:11)

A hot-tempered person must pay the penalty; rescue them, and you will have to do it again.

(Proverbs 19:19)

Mockers stir up a city, but the wise turn away anger.

(Proverbs 29:8)

Solomon declares in the last part of Proverbs 29:8 that a wise man turns away anger. The desire of the Holy Spirit is for us to learn how to deal with anger. He wants us to be "wise men," not "wise guys"! But even among believers, the sad truth is that turning away from anger is not a routine activity in today's culture!

Part Four: Abigail the Peacemaker

Just when things were about to get ugly, Abigail, the wife of Nabal, entered the picture. She is described as *"an intelligent and beautiful woman"* (1 Samuel 25:3). It is beyond me how this beautiful woman ended up marrying this ugly, nasty, mean, cruel old jerk!

As soon as Abigail heard the report of what her pathetic husband did, she immediately took action. Her beauty and intelligence will both figure prominently in her role as a peacemaker.

Abigail acted quickly. She took two hundred loaves of bread, two skins of wine, five dressed sheep, five seahs of roasted grain, a hundred cakes of raisins and two hundred cakes of pressed figs, and loaded them on donkeys. Then she told her servants, "Go on ahead; I'll follow you." But she did not tell her husband Nabal.

(1 Samuel 25:18-19)

Happy is the man who has an Abigail in his life. She defused the situation and temporarily saved her foolish husband from death. Watch the progression of her wisdom:

- She honored David by calling him "my Lord" at least eight times (see 1 Samuel 25:24-31).

- She spoke to his future, not his past (see 1 Samuel 25:30).

- She spoke to the "king" inside of David, not the "fool" who was about to go deeper into sin by killing Nabal and his men.

- She reminded David that his life was safe in God's hands and it was not worth the killing of her petty and insolent husband.

Abigail's wisdom overtook David's emotional response to Nabal's refusal. Nabal had no idea how close he was to his head becoming a permanent part of David's trophy case!

> David said to Abigail, "Praise be to the Lord, the God of Israel, who has sent you today to meet me. May you be blessed for your good judgment and for keeping me from bloodshed this day and from avenging myself with my own hands."
>
> (1 Samuel 25:32-33)

After the crisis subsided, Abigail went home and informed Nabal that she had given provisions to David. After hearing what Abigail had done (and how close he was to death), Nabal had a heart attack and died ten days later (see 1 Samuel 25:38). When David heard about Nabal's death, he sent a marriage proposal to Abigail, and she said yes (1 Samuel 25:39-42)!

WHAT CAN WE LEARN?

1. We Can Choose to Be a Victor—Not a Victim

David was about to become a victim of his uncontrolled anger. Had he not made the right choice, he would have been remembered more for the murder of Nabal than for being a "man after God's own heart"!

Dealing with anger is always a matter of choice. Whether it is suppressed anger or the constant outburst of rage, you can choose to stay a victim or be victorious. Spend time in the Proverbs and allow Solomon to be your anger management counselor and give you practical advice on how to be an overcomer.

When faced with a situation like David's, it's always best to slow down and investigate the situation before making a decision that will cost us the rest of our lives (see Proverbs 14:29; 18:13; James 1:19).

2. We Can Choose to Forgive

Not all offenses are based on false information; sometimes, they are genuine. It could result from a painful divorce, an abusive childhood, or an unnecessary termination. The pain is real, and the injury hurts. God in His wisdom has given us a surgical procedure to heal the major wounds we suffer—*forgiveness* (see Proverbs 24:29; 19:11; Ephesians 4:32).

Remember, forgiveness is not approving or agreeing that the injury is justified. Forgiveness is not synonymous with denying or even minimizing the hurt. On the contrary, just as Joseph forgave his brothers for selling him into slavery, he did not ignore their injustice or sweep it under the rug. Instead, he was blunt about what they did and confronted them with the issue: *"You intended to harm me, but God intended it for good"* (Genesis 50:20).

Solomon tells us that overlooking a transgression is to a person's glory. The word *overlook* means to "set aside or go beyond." The Hebrew word for *forgiveness* means "to release." True forgiveness means that we must be willing to release them from their responsibility for the hurt they have caused. Forgiveness isn't a feeling or a word; it's a choice, and Solomon is emphatic when he says that when you make that choice, you will receive glory!

3. We Can Choose to Be a Peacemaker, Not a Peacebreaker

Abigail chose to defuse the situation and thus became a peacemaker. She was the embodiment of Matthew 5:9, which says, *"Blessed are the peacemakers, for they will be called children of God."* She also knew that the relationship was more important than the issue.

> The more we run from conflict, the more it masters us; the more we try to avoid it, the more it controls us. The less we fear conflict, the less it confuses us; the less we deny our differences, the less they divide us.
>
> —David Augsburger[5]

When working toward a solution, consider Philippians 2:4-5:

Not looking to your own interests but each of you to the interests of the others. In your relationships with one another, have the same mindset as Christ Jesus.

Seek solutions that keep everyone's best interests in mind, so that rather than becoming a peacebreaker, you will become a peacemaker.

NOTES

1. Groucho Marx, qtd. in Eve Starr, "Inside TV," *Greensboro Record,* November 3, 1954, https://quoteinvestigator.com/2014/05/17/angry-speech.

2. Charles R. Swindoll, *David: A Man of Passion and Destiny,* 158-159.

3. Alan Redpath, *The Making of a Man of God,* 107.

4. https://sermons.faithlife.com/sermons/10874-1-samuel-25:1-44-the-offense-of-nabal/ accessed August 12, 2022.

5. David Augsburger, *Conflict Mediation Across Cultures* (Louisville, KY: John Knox Press, 1992), 229.

8

LIFE IN THE PITS

I find myself frequently depressed in spirit—perhaps more so than any other person here—and I find no better cure for that depression than to trust in the Lord with all my heart and seek to realize afresh the power of the peace-speaking blood of Jesus and His Infinite Love in dying upon the Cross to put away all my transgressions.

—Charles Spurgeon[1]

But David thought to himself, "One of these days I will be destroyed by the hand of Saul. The best thing I can do is to escape to the land of the Philistines. Then Saul will give up searching for me anywhere in Israel, and I will slip out of his hand." So David and the six hundred men with him left and went over to Achish son of Maok king of Gath. David and his men settled in Gath with Achish. Each man had his family with him, and David had his two wives: Ahinoam of Jezreel and Abigail of Carmel, the widow of Nabal. When Saul was told that David had fled to Gath, he no longer searched for him.

—1 Samuel 27:1-4

INTRODUCTION

Davavid was still on the run. He moved from cave to cave, hiding from Saul and his men. I can imagine there came the point in the wilderness experience when David said to himself, "I'm so tired of running—when will it end?"

A casual reading of 1 Samuel 26 and 27 shows us that David was not only running from Saul but also fighting invisible enemies. There are times when the invisible can be more dangerous than the visible. Just who were these insidious enemies? Something we have all faced: *discouragement and depression.*

No one is immune. It doesn't matter if you have been a believer for forty years or four months; the twin killers of joy and motivation can strike without warning. As a believer, I can attest that discouragement and depression have become occupational hazards many people face, especially leaders.

There is no shame in finding yourself in the pit of depression and discouragement. It can happen to the best of us. The issue becomes more serious when we decide there is no hope of getting out of the pit and resign ourselves to a life of misery and hopelessness.

One thing I do know is when these evil twins invade our life, it makes even daily living difficult. Frequent occurrences of depression can lead to a loss of joy and zest for living. Instead of living our life in the bright sunshine of God's love and beauty, everything around us turns dull, gray, and lifeless. For many, depression is debilitating, even to the point of suicide.

Depression is one of the world's most common health conditions. It's estimated that one-in-three women and one-in-five men have an episode of major depression by the age of 65.[2]

That adds up to roughly 54 million women and 33 million men in America who will be seriously depressed at some point in their lives. The disorder is so common that it is called the common cold of mental illness.

Keep in mind that David had already won several victories. He listened to the wise counsel of Abigail and won the battle over his uncontrolled anger (see 1 Samuel 25). He refused to kill Saul when he had the chance (see 1 Samuel 24–26). He knew the taste of victory.

But now, we see David in the pit. He did not suddenly or accidentally fall into the pit of depression, discouragement, and despair. No, it never seems to work that way. It took a series of events to land him in such a dark and foreboding place. He made several bad choices—and it cost him many days and nights of wandering through the wilderness of confusion and inner turmoil.

HOW DID DAVID END UP IN THE PIT?

David Chose Doubt Instead of God's Promises

In 1 Samuel 26, David had another opportunity to kill Saul. While the king and his men were sleeping, David took Saul's spear and a water jug to prove how close he could get to the king. Even though his men wanted David to kill Saul, David refused to *"lay a hand on the Lord's anointed"* (1 Samuel 26:23). David was bound by his honor and commitment to the king. And this was despite all Saul had done to eliminate David from the face of the earth.

After Saul discovered what David had done, he offered forgiveness a second time, but David knew better. David knew of Saul's jealousy and that he would go to his grave wanting to see David dead. David was trying to make things right. He was doing everything he knew to fix the problem, but nothing worked. Nothing he could do would keep Saul from trying to kill him, which drove him deeper into the dark pit of despair.

> *But David thought to himself, "One of these days I will be destroyed by the hand of Saul. The best thing I can do is to escape to the land of the Philistines. Then Saul will give up searching for me anywhere in Israel, and I will slip out of his hand."*

> (1 Samuel 27:1)

G. Campbell Morgan said, "David's sense of his danger increased until he became almost pessimistic, and he said in his heart, 'I shall now perish one day by the hand of Saul.' And who can wonder at, or blame him? Long and weary indeed had been his period of suffering."[3]

It's not that David stopped believing in God. He allowed doubt to cloud his mind and make him think that God would not do what He said He would do—make him king.

Doubt is the opposite of faith, and it will diminish our confidence in God's purpose for our life. Worry usually follows doubt. When you worry about what God said He would do to take care of you, that is the same as suggesting that you have more intellect than God.

> To deal with our doubts about God, we must make an intentional shift from being self-centered to faith-centered. No matter what it looks like, we can still trust God to be faithful and know that He does what is best for our life.
>
> —Unknown

There is a world of difference in believing in God and believing God's Word. The real test of our faith is not believing that there is a God, but believing in God's promises. Just believing in God is *not* enough. Remember, the demons believe in God, but that does not make them Christian (see James 2:19).

David panicked, and his panic led him into a bottomless pit of depression. Saul came after David with 3,000 chosen men (see 1 Samuel 26:2), which meant David had a problem that would not go away. You get tired and discouraged when you have a problem that will not go away, whether it is sickness, issues at work, or financial difficulties. If you are not careful, you will slide into a depressed spirit, wake up one day, and realize you see only darkness. Wishing and hoping will not make it go away. Action has to be taken, or it will eat you alive.

The apostle Paul knew all about suffering and pain. Deep within a Roman prison, he shared the secret to winning the war over worry, depression, and discouragement. He said:

> *Rejoice in the Lord always. I will say it again: Rejoice! Let your gentleness be evident to all. The Lord is near.* **Do not be anxious about anything, but in every situation, by prayer and petition, with thanksgiving, present your requests to God.** *And the peace of God, which transcends all understanding, will guard your hearts and your minds in Christ Jesus.*
>
> (Philippians 4:4-7)

He didn't say, "Don't worry, be happy." Instead, he said, "Don't worry—pray about everything, and let God handle things!"

David Chose Feelings over Faith

I have learned through challenging experiences that focusing on how you feel rather than the facts of God's Word can cause depression. There have been times when I have felt that God had deserted me. Maybe you have too. Emotions and feelings will never give you an accurate picture of God's actions. Our emotions are like elevators—they go up and down at the push of a button. But God is ever faithful, and according to Numbers 23:19-20:

God is not human, that he should lie, not a human being, that he should change his mind. Does he speak and then not act? Does he promise and not fulfill? I have received a command to bless; he has blessed, and I cannot change it.

If you get to the point where you feel God has deserted you and there is no hope, you have to shake yourself and realize that God's Word is true and His promises are *yes* and *amen*. Deuteronomy 31:8 says, "*The Lord himself goes before you and will be with you; he will never leave you nor forsake you. Do not be afraid; do not be discouraged.*" That verse excited me because the Bible says God will not leave us. No matter how bad the circumstances or how bad your problem is, God is right there beside you when the enemy attacks you.

Over one hundred verses in Scripture tell me that God knew me before I was born. That means God had a plan for our life before we came into existence. For instance:

Listen to me, you islands; hear this, you distant nations: before I was born the Lord called me; from my mother's womb he has spoken my name.

(Isaiah 49:1)

The word of the Lord came to me, saying, "Before I formed you in the womb I knew you, before you were born I set you apart; I appointed you as a prophet to the nations."

(Jeremiah 1:4-5)

For you created my inmost being; you knit me together in my mother's womb. I praise you because I am fearfully and wonderfully made; your works are wonderful, I know that full well. My frame was not hidden from you when I was made in the secret place, when I was woven together in the depths of the earth. Your eyes saw my unformed body; all the days ordained for me were written in your book before one of them came to be.

(Psalm 139:13-16)

For we are God's handiwork, created in Christ Jesus to do good works, which God prepared in advance for us to do.

(Ephesians 2:10)

All David could think about was how he felt, not God's promises. If David would only have stopped to think about how God had been faithful to him in the past!

Oh, David, don't you remember how God delivered you from the lion and the bear? Don't you remember how God delivered Goliath into your hand? And, most importantly, don't you remember that it was God who chose you to be the future king of Israel?

David's short-term memory lapse caused him to focus on his problems and an enemy that would not go away. It caused him to focus on feelings rather than God.

David Chose to Run from His Problem

And where did David run? To the enemy's camp!

> *But David thought to himself, "One of these days I will be destroyed by the hand of Saul. The best thing I can do is to escape to the land of the Philistines. Then Saul will give up searching for me anywhere in Israel, and I will slip out of his hand."*
>
> *So David and the six hundred men with him left and went over to Achish son of Maok king of Gath. David and his men settled in Gath with Achish. Each man had his family with him, and David had his two wives: Ahinoam of Jezreel and Abigail of Carmel, the widow of Nabal. When Saul was told that David had fled to Gath, he no longer searched for him.*
>
> *Then David said to Achish, "If I have found favor in your eyes, let a place be assigned to me in one of the country towns, that I may live there. Why should your servant live in the royal city with you?"*
>
> *So on that day Achish gave him Ziklag, and it has belonged to the kings of Judah ever since.*
>
> (1 Samuel 27:1-6)

David's choices had dire consequences. They created an atmosphere of gloom, doom, and despair making everything look bleak. I do not believe depression is a sin, but it can take you there. When you are depressed and discouraged, you forget the things of God and move into areas you usually would never go.

Because of David's depression, he turned to an enemy instead of turning toward God. David's new best friend was none other than Achish, the son of the king of Gath. Where have we heard of that place before? Well, it was none other than the hometown of Goliath.

David's new best friend gave him and his band of men a city, Ziklag, to use as a base of operations. From there they conducted guerrilla raids:

> *Now David and his men went up and raided the Geshurites, the Girzites and the Amalekites. (From ancient times these peoples had lived in the land extending to Shur and Egypt.) Whenever David attacked an area, he did not leave a man or woman alive, but took sheep and cattle, donkeys and camels, and clothes. Then he returned to Achish.*
>
> (1 Samuel 27:8-9)

When asked by Achish about his activities, he lied and told him he was only raiding Israeli cities. What made these massacres even worse was that he was not doing it to protect the armies of Israel or his army. David was doing all of this for his benefit, not anyone else. David had allowed depression to control his life, and he sank deeper and deeper into sin. Looking for relief in all the wrong places when dealing with problems is very easy. And when relief does not show up, we are tempted to do just what David did. It is a vicious cycle, and no one is immune.

To defeat depression, you have to stop focusing on feelings and start focusing on the facts of the Word. The process will begin when you allow Philippians 4:8 to become your focal point:

> *Finally, brothers and sisters, whatever is true, whatever is noble, whatever is right, whatever is pure, whatever is lovely, whatever is admirable—if anything is excellent or praiseworthy—think about such things.*

David's biggest mistake was focusing more on his circumstances than God who could do something about them. He lived "under" the weight of his problems and allowed his depression and discouragement to rule his emotions. His actions proved he forgot things that were *true, noble, right, pure, admirable, and praiseworthy*. And when David forgot to remember the faithfulness of God, sin was lying at the door!

WHAT CAN WE LEARN?

1. The Bible Does Not Avoid the Subject of Depression and Discouragement

It should be no surprise that the Bible has much to say about issues affecting our daily lives. Some (if not all) of the greatest heroes of the faith dealt with some form of depression and discouragement. Think about Moses, Elijah, Peter, Paul, and even the hero of our story, David.

Yes, even the man who was "after God's own heart" dealt with emotional issues.

> The Bible is not full of men and women who are immune or unaware of what it's like to experience sorrow and pain. God included and made sure that these true stories were included in the Bible, partly so that you would know you're not alone. Depression can come for anyone.[4]

If you are unsure how prevalent depression was, all you have to do is spend some time reading the Psalms. Many of them were written while David was in the depths of depression and despair.

On more than one occasion, this "sweet singer of Israel" sounded like a man who lost his faith entirely. He said in Psalm 42:3-5:

> *My tears have been my food day and night, while people say to me all day long, "Where is your God?" These things I remember as I pour out my soul: how I used to go to the house of God under the protection of the Mighty One with shouts of joy and praise among the festive throng. Why, my soul, are you downcast? Why so disturbed within me? Put your hope in God, for I will yet praise him, my Savior and my God.*

And in Psalm 6:6-7 David lamented:

I am worn out from my groaning. All night long I flood my bed with weeping and drench my couch with tears. My eyes grow weak with sorrow; they fail because of all my foes.

David, downcast and discouraged from his struggles with his enemies, had come to the end of himself.

The good news is, he did not stay dejected and downhearted because he learned how to seek God to renew his spirit. He knew his hope and help was only found in God! (More on that in the next chapter!)

I have to say David isn't just writing about his own experiences. He is describing something many lovers of Jesus face at some point in their lifetime. If we don't learn the lessons that David learned, we will face the constant spirit of discouragement and depression.

The reality of depression and discouragement is no respecter of persons. In the Christian life, there are mountaintops and valleys. It seems that the mountaintop experiences don't last as long as we think they should. I am not trying to be facetious; it just seems the mountaintop is there to give a little encouragement and prepare you to spend more time in the valley. But there is a place in God where you do not have to ride the roller coaster of depression and discouragement. What we have to remember is that God is with us in the valleys as well as on the mountaintops.

2. Don't Allow the Enemy to Drive a Wedge Between You and God

Remember how David's downward spiral started?

> *But David thought to himself, "One of these days I will be destroyed by the hand of Saul. The best thing I can do is to escape to the land of the Philistines. Then Saul will give up searching for me anywhere in Israel, and I will slip out of his hand."*

(1 Samuel 27:1)

Can you hear the negative talk? David allowed the pressure of his circumstances to drive a wedge between him and God's promises. Instead of seeking the Lord as he did in other times of difficulty, David was filled with negativity and doubt.

David allowed his depression to cause him to be paranoid and fearful. He had gone so far as to feel God was hiding from him and the closeness of fellowship with God was gone. He said in Psalm 10:1: *"Why, Lord, do you stand far off? Why do you hide yourself in times of trouble?"* That's why depression and discouragement are so dangerous—they separate us from the reality of God's Word.

When allowed to fester, these evil twins will cause us to lose the sense of fellowship with God. We walk away from God one step at a time when that happens. That's why Isaiah wrote: *"But your iniquities have separated you from your God; your sins have hidden his face from you, so that he will not hear"* (Isaiah 59:2). When discouragement and

LIFE IN THE PITS

depression lead us into sin, our prayers cannot be answered. The Bible tells us in Psalm 66:18: *"If I had cherished sin in my heart, the Lord would not have listened."*

3. Discover Your Hope Is in the Lord

Marshall Segal wrote:

> While many are lost to their depression—helplessly wandering in their own darkness—Christians have somewhere to turn, truths to rehearse until our hearts catch up with the faith in our minds. Not only did Christ save and deliver the brokenhearted, but he experienced all the pains and temptations we face and more. At the cross, he dove headfirst into the darkness, so that we might have eternal, unfading, always-increasing hope and happiness.[5]

Isaiah 61:1-3 outlines how to move from depression to freedom. It begins and ends with a relationship with the Lord.

> *The Spirit of the Sovereign Lord is on me, because the Lord has anointed me to proclaim good news to the poor. He has sent me to bind up the brokenhearted, to proclaim freedom for the captives and release from darkness for the prisoners, to proclaim the year of the Lord's favor and the day of vengeance of our God, to comfort all who mourn, and provide for those who grieve in Zion—to bestow on them a crown of beauty instead of ashes, the oil of joy instead of mourning, and a garment of praise instead of a spirit of despair. They*

will be called oaks of righteousness, a planting of the Lord for the display of his splendor.

Read that Scripture again and pick out the words that describe what the pit looks like—*brokenhearted, captive, darkness, mourning, grieving, ashes,* and *despair.* That doesn't sound like a fun place!

Now go back and reread it and see what the Lord will do for those who want to leave the pit and walk with Him in freedom and joy—*good news, bind up, freedom, release, favor, comfort, oil of joy, garment of praise.*

The Lord will do all that and more for those who want to break the shackles of pain and darkness!

NOTES

1. Charles Spurgeon, "The Secret of Happiness," The Metropolitan Tabernacle, Newington, May 2, 1872, https://ccel.org/ccel/spurgeon/sermons56/sermons56.l.html.

2. Saloni Dattani, "What is the lifetime risk of depression?" OurWorldInData.org, May 18, 2022, https://ourworldindata.org/depression-lifetime-risk.

3. G. Campbell Morgan, *An Exposition of the Whole Bible* (Old Tappan, New Jersey: Fleming H. Revell, 1959), 125.

4. David Marvin and Laura Eldredge, "5 People in the Bible Who Struggled with Depression," The Porch.live, August 28, 2020, https://www.theporch.live/blog/5-people-in-the-bible-who-struggled-with-depression.

5. Article by Marshall Segal, "Too Depressed to Believe What We Know," DesiringGod.org, July 14, 2015, https://www.desiringgod.org/articles/too-depressed-to-believe-what-we-know.

Section III

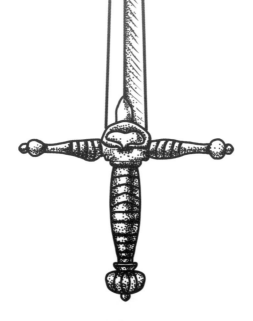

WARRIORS IN
TRIUMPH

9

THE ROAD TO RECOVERY

The Christian life is not a life of clear sailing. Every believer is going to have bad days, no matter how holy he may be. In fact, I believe the more godly a person is, the more trying and excruciating his bad days will be.

—David Wilkerson[1]

David and his men reached Ziklag on the third day. Now the Amalekites had raided the Negev and Ziklag. They had attacked Ziklag and burned it, and had taken captive the women and everyone else in it, both young and old. They killed none of them, but carried them off as they went on their way.

—1 Samuel 30:1-2

INTRODUCTION

There is something about coming home after being away for an extended period. Any time spent away from family is more bearable because we know we can go home again at some point.

That feeling must have invigorated David and his mighty men as they headed back to their temporary base of operations in Ziklag.

You remember it was Achish, the son of the king of Gath (Goliath's hometown), who gave David and his roving band of men a place to base their guerilla war against the Amalekites (see 1 Samuel 27:1-6). David thought he could avoid his nemesis (Saul) by hiding in enemy territory. David's reasoning to hide where his enemy was lodged was faulty at best and costly and dangerous at its worst. David would have been better served to run toward the Lord instead of running away from Saul and living in the enemy's camp! *There are bad days, and there are really, really bad days. David was about to have one of the latter!*

As David and his men approached the city, they immediately noticed something was wrong (see 1 Samuel 30:1-3). Instead of the usual greeting from their families, all they saw was smoke rising from what looked like burned-out buildings. To their horror, they discovered that the Amalekites came into their unprotected camp while they were away and burned it to the ground. And there was more shock to come—the enemy had taken captive their wives, including David's two wives, and their sons and daughters.

It has been suggested that this raid by the Amalekites was payback for what David had done. The saying "what goes around comes around" could be applied here. David had hit rock bottom. As Alan Redpath pointed out:

> It is indeed true that the darkest hour in a man's experience
> is always just before the dawning of new light. Well, might
> David say at this point, "The cords of death entangled me;
> the torrents of destruction overwhelmed me. The cords

of the grave coiled around me; the snares of death confronted me" (Psalm 18:4-5).[2]

This chapter in the life of David and his men could have two possible endings. On the one hand, David could give in to his grief and allow his men (who were so distraught) to do whatever they wanted to do to him, or David could use this tragedy as a springboard to a renewed trust in the promises of God.

Thank God David chose the latter and made the right decision. He learned how to refocus on the promises of God and *not* on a burned-out city and his men who wanted to kill him! The theme of 1 Samuel 30 is not how much David lost but how much he gained by trusting God in his hour of distress. The Lord told David that he *"will certainly overtake them and succeed in the rescue"* (1 Samuel 30:8).

David plotted a course of action that progressively led him from tragedy to triumph. David's following *four steps* are a "pattern" for us when sudden terror strikes our hearts. Proverbs 3:25-26 says:

> ***Have no fear of sudden disaster*** *or of the ruin that overtakes the wicked, for the Lord will be at your side and will keep your foot from being snared.*

FOUR STEPS TO RECOVER IT ALL

1. David Wept

When the men rode into the city and realized the devastation, they *"wept aloud until they had no strength left to weep"* (1 Samuel 30:4).

- David and his men saw the city's devastation and wept.
- David saw the grief on the faces of his men and he wept.
- David realized his family had been taken captive and wept.
- David felt alone and afraid and wept.

David and his men cried until there was no more strength to weep. They were, as we say, "all cried out"!

Is it wrong for a believer to show emotions? Allisen Shawver of NorthShore Church writes:

> This story highlights one of the most gut-wrenching chapters in David's life and it also reveals many truths about God and how he works in the lives of his people in times of great trauma and stress. This story reveals how to respond in times of trial and enemy attack and our goal... is to be strengthened in God through these truths.[3]

In our culture, we (especially men) are told that weeping is a sign of weakness or a lack of character. In the movie *A League of Their Own*, there is a now-famous quote: "There is no crying in baseball." It was screamed by Jimmy Dugan (Tom Hanks) to his outfielder Evelyn

Gardner (Bitty Schram), who failed to make a play. Hank's character said, in essence, that we need to keep a "stiff upper lip," as the British are fond of saying. In other words, please don't allow anyone to see us in such a vulnerable state.

Sometimes in our life, our tears are not a sign of weakness but reveal our brokenness before the Lord. God did not create us to be puppets or robots. We are made in the likeness of our Creator, and our heavenly Father put a wide range of emotions within us, including the capacity to weep.

Even the Lord Jesus wept at the tomb of Lazarus. John 11:33-36 says:

> *When Jesus saw her weeping, and the Jews who had come along with her also weeping, he was deeply moved in spirit and troubled. "Where have you laid him?" he asked." Come and see, Lord," they replied. **Jesus wept**. Then the Jews said, "See how he loved him!"*

In his excellent book *What to Do on the Worst Day of Your Life*, Brian Zahnd said:

> Stoicism has nothing to do with faith. Living by faith is not living without feelings. Being strong in faith does not make us immune to emotion. Those who live by faith experience emotion like everybody else—they just don't allow emotion to have the last word. God has created us as emotional beings; it is part of our human nature. Emotions are an essential part of experiencing pleasure and joy

in life. Those who deny their emotional makeup become people with bland personalities incapable of really enjoying life. To deny true sorrow is also to deny true joy. Having a flat, prosaic personality is not what it means to be a person of faith.[4]

There are times when circumstances are so devastating that the only thing we can do is weep until there is no more strength left in us. But we must remember what David so eloquently said in Psalm 30:5, *"Weeping may stay for the night, but rejoicing comes in the morning."*

Yes, David cried his eyes out, but that's not the end of the story. Not by a long shot. He dried his tears and determined to do something to rectify the situation.

2. David Waited

The situation was getting tense. I can picture the scene: David's men dried their eyes, turned toward their leader, and said, "Let's stone him—he's responsible for this mess!"

> *David was greatly distressed because the men were talking of stoning him; each one was bitter in spirit because of his sons and daughters. But David found strength in the Lord his God.*
>
> (1 Samuel 30:6)

While his men were looking for rocks to throw, David didn't panic or try to defend himself. I find no evidence that David spoke to the men at all. He didn't gather the men and shout, "Listen, guys, I know I messed up, so instead of stoning me, let's try to work through this tragedy." That didn't happen. David already knew that things had gone south, so he didn't need anyone (especially the men he trained) to tell him how bad things were. David already knew, and he didn't need reminding.

David did one of the most challenging things any of us can do—he waited. Our natural inclination (especially men) is to hurry and try to fix whatever is broken. It's that urge to do something *now* that often leads to trouble.

Strong leaders tend to "shoot first and ask questions later." Waiting before acting is not one of our most inherent character traits. Taking action when our emotions are overloaded is the quickest way to make the biggest mistake in judgment. We need to heed the words of Moses when it would seem he was at a place of certain doom with Egyptians behind him and the Red Sea in front:

*Moses answered the people, "Do not be afraid. **Stand firm** and you will see the deliverance the Lord will bring you today. The Egyptians you see today you will never see again. The Lord will fight for you; you need **only to be still**."*

(Exodus 14:13-14)

Several psalms indicate that David, like Moses, knew the importance of waiting before the Lord. Many of these psalms were written during the wilderness years and reflect David's desire for God to move in his circumstances.

Wait for the Lord; be strong and take heart and wait for the Lord.

(Psalm 27:14)

Be still before the Lord and wait patiently for him; do not fret when people succeed in their ways, when they carry out their wicked schemes.

(Psalm 37:7)

Lord, I wait for you; you will answer, Lord my God.

(Psalm 38:15)

David's waiting was not without a purpose: *"He encouraged himself in the Lord."* How did he encourage himself in the Lord when everything around him screamed discouragement, loss, and ruin? He changed his focus from defeat to victory, and suddenly an impossible situation was about to be turned around. There may come a time when there is no one who will encourage us. No one to talk to or shoulder to cry on—no help in sight. Remember, when it's just you and the Lord (no matter how terrible things look), you are in the majority every time!

Out of the depths of despair, David made a decision. I can almost hear him as he cries, "I will no longer be a captive to my circumstances. I will *not* let go of my calling and destiny in the Lord. I have the anointing of a king, and I will start acting like a king!"

David didn't give up; he looked up. As you continue to read through the entire chapter, you can see the transformation in David's attitude.

3. David Worshiped and Prayed

First Samuel 30:7-8 declares:

> *Then David said to Abiathar the priest, the son of Ahimelek, "Bring me the ephod." Abiathar brought it to him, and David inquired of the Lord, "Shall I pursue this raiding party? Will I overtake them?" "Pursue them," he answered. "You will certainly overtake them and succeed in the rescue."*

David's problems began when he put prayer on the shelf. He made critical decisions in his life without consulting God. The Lord wants to be our source. He desires to talk to us about every aspect of our life. When we let God become our source, He is faithful and will never let our steps waver.

The first lesson we need to learn when in a desperate situation is to stop everything—*wait, worship, and pray!*

David needed direction. A renewed vision. David didn't gather his men and ask their opinion on what to do next. There may be circumstances when we need to gain a consensus from those on our team. But David knew something—if he wanted direction from the Lord, he would have to avoid the crowd's chattering voices. The last thing he wanted was the "noise" to drown out the "still small voice of the Lord."

Joyce Meyer wrote in *The Battle Belongs to the Lord*:

> We should develop the habit of running to God when we have trouble instead of to people. We should seek God

rather than our own minds and other people's minds. Ask yourself, "When trouble comes, do I run to the phone or to the throne?" God might direct us to a person for advice, but we should always go to Hm first to show that we honor and trust Him.[5]

David said to Abiathar, *"Bring me the ephod."* He said, in so many words, "I must hear from God." When David needed a word from the Lord, he would lay aside his weapons of war and put on an ephod, or a priest's garment. Interestingly, the last time we saw David inquire of the Lord utilizing the ephod was in 1 Samuel 23:9:

> *When David learned that Saul was plotting against him, he said to Abiathar the priest, "Bring the ephod."*

This is the first time since 1 Samuel 26 that David has called on the name of the Lord. That tells me that it took a horrendous situation to cause David to look to the Lord again for his needed help.

Through prayer, David received a "now" word from God. "No matter how long it takes, I'm not coming out from under the prayer covering until I hear from God," was his attitude.

"Shall I pursue this raiding party? Will I overtake them?" was David's simple question. And the Lord answered: "Pursue them. You will certainly overtake them and succeed in the rescue."

4. David Won

"You will recover it all!" must have been music to David's ears. The time for worship and prayer was over—he received the word he needed, and now it was time to take action. David strapped on his weapons and told his fighting force of six hundred men, "Let's go and recover all that the enemy has stolen!"

There is a time to weep, wait, worship, and pray, but there is also a time to go to war and take back what the enemy has taken from us!

In David's day, it was a physical battle. Men against men fought to the death to recover all the enemy had taken.

> *David fought them from dusk until the evening of the next day, and none of them got away, except four hundred young men who rode off on camels and fled. David **recovered everything the Amalekites had taken, including his two wives.** Nothing was missing: young or old, boy or girl, plunder or anything else they had taken. David brought everything back. He took all the flocks and herds, and his men drove them ahead of the other livestock, saying, **"This is David's plunder."***
>
> (1 Samuel 30:17-20)

The victory was secure. As David moved forward with a victory in hand, he was no longer running from the enemy but acting like a king ready to reign!

———◆———

WHAT CAN WE LEARN?

1. Bad Days Happen to Everyone

No one is immune from having a bad day. Not even bad days that turn into even worse bad days. When David realized what had happened in Ziklag, it would have been easy for him to fall into the pit of self-pity.

You can mark it down—when you spend more time focusing on problems instead of God's promises, you are headed for trouble. There are seven thousand promises in the Bible, and God has kept every one of them. Lamentations 3:22-23 says, *"Because of the Lord's great love we are not consumed, for his compassions never fail. They are new every morning; great is your faithfulness."* Just those two verses alone should give us reason to trust that God is faithful no matter what kind of situation in which we might find ourselves. I know He will never let us down, no matter how difficult the situation looks. We always have a choice to rebel and get bitter or repent and get better.

2. We Don't War against Flesh and Blood

Paul unmasked our *real* enemy in Ephesians 6:12:

> *For our struggle is not against flesh and blood, but against the rulers, against the authorities, against the powers of this dark world and against the spiritual forces of evil in the heavenly realms.*

The apostle Paul clarified that our warfare is not with people but with spiritual forces that seek to destroy our families, testimony, and life. The Good News is that we have been given powerful spiritual weapons to fight against the enemy.

For though we live in the world, we do not wage war as the world does. The weapons we fight with are not the weapons of the world. On the contrary, they have divine power to demolish strongholds. We demolish arguments and every pretension that sets itself up against the knowledge of God, and we take captive every thought to make it obedient to Christ. And we will be ready to punish every act of disobedience, once your obedience is complete.

(2 Corinthians 10:3-6)

- We have the *blood* of Jesus to deal with our sin (see 1 John 1:7).
- We have the *cross* of Jesus to deal with our flesh (see Romans 6:6).
- We have the *name* of Jesus to face our enemy (see Philippians 2:10-11).
- We have the *faith* of Jesus to shield us from the fiery darts of the enemy (see Ephesians 6:16).

3. Refuse to Blame Others

The reaction of David's men reminds me that those of us in positions of leadership know what it's like to have plans go wrong and end up being blamed. Leaders are easy targets. When things go downhill, just point the finger at the one in charge! What David's men did was nothing new. The "blame game" was not invented by them; instead, this insidious game started with our first parents in the Garden. (Read Genesis 3 for a complete account.)

David didn't argue with his men or turn around and accuse them for blaming him! Instead, David did what a wise leader should do: he turned his face toward the *One* who could offer help in time of need—the Lord Almighty.

The next time you encounter a bad day, don't blame others or try to figure it out yourself. Do what David did. Seek God, wait for the answer, and then take action!

Notes

1. David Wilkerson, "A Message for Christians Who Have Bad Days," WorldChallenge.org, https://www.worldchallenge.org/message -christians-who-have-bad-days.

2. Alan Redpath, *The Making of a Man of God,* 121.

3. Allisen Shawver, "The Life of David: Disaster at Ziklag," NorthShore Church, January 12, 2021, https://nshorechurch .com/2021/01/12/the-life-of-david-disaster-at-ziklag-1-10-21.

4. Brian Zahnd, *What to Do on the Worst Day of Your Life* (Lake Mary, FL: Christian Life, 2009), 8.

5. Joyce Meyer, *The Battle Belongs to the Lord* (New York, NY: Warner Books, 2002), 6.

10

THE DEATH OF AN ENEMY

I mourn the loss of thousands of precious lives, but I will not rejoice in the death of one, not even an enemy.

—Martin Luther King, Jr.[1]

Then David and all the men with him took hold of their clothes and tore them. They mourned and wept and fasted till evening for Saul and his son Jonathan, and for the army of the Lord and for the nation of Israel, because they had fallen by the sword.

—2 Samuel 1:11-12

INTRODUCTION

David and his men barely had time to celebrate their victory over the Amalekites when they received the news of Saul and Jonathan's deaths. First Samuel 31:8-10 says:

The next day, when the Philistines came to strip the dead, they found Saul and his three sons fallen on Mount Gilboa.

They cut off his head and stripped off his armor, and they sent messengers throughout the land of the Philistines to proclaim the news in the temple of their idols and among their people. They put his armor in the temple of the Ashtoreths and fastened his body to the wall of Beth Shan.

What a startling contrast. While David was sharing the spoils with those men who stayed behind (see 1 Samuel 30:23-26), Saul and his sons were being stripped on the battlefield!

God abandoned Saul, and the only thing left for the disobedient king was the judgment of death. It is sad that the mountain that gave Israel victories (see Judges 4,5,7) now became the scene of horrible defeat and slaughter.

An Amalekite brought the news of Saul's death to David (see 2 Samuel 1:5-15). He even brought Saul's crown and bracelet to David for proof. He claimed to be the one who finally took Saul's life. This would not have happened if Saul had obeyed the word of the Lord in 1 Samuel 15 and killed all Amalekites. *The sin we fail to eliminate today has the potential to rise and kill us tomorrow!*

If there was ever a misreading of someone's character, it had to be this poor Amalekite who thought David would reward him for killing King Saul. While he seemed to be bragging about his actions, he was signing his death warrant. He was expecting to hear David say, "Good job, you can stay here and live with us," but instead, David turned to one of his men and said, "Take him out and kill him!"

David was no fool. The issue for David was as straightforward as it could be. But this Amalekite saw it differently. This guy thought David viewed Saul as his enemy, someone who stood in his way to the throne. Regardless of Saul's disobedience and how many times he tried to kill David, it did not matter to David. In his mind, it was a simple and clear-cut matter. *You killed the Lord's anointed, and now you must pay the price.*

—————◆◆◆—————

How Did David React When His Enemy Fell?

How do you suppose David would react when he heard the news of the death of his greatest antagonist? No doubt a lesser man would have celebrated that his enemy was killed. David didn't rejoice but demonstrated he was indeed a man after God's heart. He was deeply moved when he heard the news: *"They mourned and wept and fasted till evening for Saul and his son Jonathan, and for the army of the Lord and for the nation of Israel, because they had fallen by the sword"* (2 Samuel 1:12). Included in the distressing news was the death of his covenant friend Jonathan. It is tragic when the sin of a disobedient father brings judgment upon an innocent son.

David's attitude about how we should respond when an enemy falls is revealed in two ways:

1. David Refused to Rejoice

Proverbs 24:17-18 tells us what to do when an enemy falls: *"Do not gloat when your enemy falls; when they stumble, do not let your heart rejoice, or the Lord will see and disapprove and turn his wrath away from them."*

Instead of gloating, David grieved.

Instead of criticizing, he eulogized.

David refused to rejoice because he knew only God could remove a man from office. It would've been easy for David to say, "He got what he deserved!" But he refused to say anything critical or unkind about Saul. David would not berate a man or woman of God.

A modern-day example of David's attitude was Dr. Martin Luther King, Jr. Those who wanted to destroy him often put his commitment to nonviolence to the test. On many occasions, Dr. King found himself the object of violence. To say that King had enemies would be a significant understatement. The opportunity was abundant for him to respond in kind, but he chose to walk a different path. King refused to live by the "eye for eye" code of revenge.

One of the earliest attempts on his life occurred on January 30, 1956. A bomb was thrown on the front porch of his home in Montgomery, Alabama. He was away at the time, but his wife and baby were inside. Fortunately, they were unharmed, and only a small amount of damage was done to the house. How did Dr. King respond?

> The explosion outraged the community and was a major test of King's steadfast commitment to non-violence. ... News of the bombing spread quickly, and an angry crowd

soon gathered outside King's home. A matter of minutes after his home had been bombed, standing feet away from the site of the explosion, King preached non-violence. "I want you to love our enemies," he told his supporters. "Be good to them, love them, and let them know you love them." It was a prime example of King's deeply-held belief in nonviolence, as what could have been a riot instead became a powerful display of the highest ideals of the civil rights movement.[2]

David, like Dr. King, had plenty of opportunities to seek out those who would do him harm. He refused to sink to the lowest level of human interaction and take revenge on his enemies.

What should our reaction be when someone falls (friend or foe)? It may not be so drastic as physical death (like Saul), but whatever the failure turns out to be, should we gloat or spread the news?

Pastor John Lawrence made an interesting observation when discussing how we should respond when an enemy falls:

> When we are walking with God, we will have enemies. That is a given in our fallen world. But when God displays His anger toward someone—we should not be on the sidelines cheering for their judgment. We can cheer God's justice—but we should do so with a measure of fear and trembling. The reason for this is because we need to remember who *we* are.
>
> We are beneficiaries of God's mercy—not His judgment. If God were to judge us for our actions—we would quickly

learn that we too, apart from His grace, are His enemies. There is something to grasp—and it is important that we keep it fresh in our minds. Were it not for what God did in Jesus Christ, we would be under His wrath and anger as well. It is only because of Jesus Christ and His death on the cross that we are not currently under God's anger. Therefore, we do not need to rejoice when our enemy stumbles and falls. We need to remember that except for the grace of God, we would be enemies as well.[3]

Christians are the only army in the world that kills its wounded, and it's time to stop! It seems in the Church we get some sort of twisted pleasure when a brother or sister is overtaken in sin. If you want to crank up the rumor mill just start a whisper campaign about someone in the congregation.

I pray that Christians adopt the same attitude as the U.S. Armed Forces. For over two hundred years, our fighting men have stated they will leave no one on the battlefield—alive, dead, or wounded, all are coming home. Even the Greeks portrayed heroes as those who rescued those captured by enemies.

David's behavior exemplified the very essence of Paul, who wrote in Galatians 6:1, "*Brothers and sisters, if someone is caught in a sin, you who live by the Spirit should restore that person gently. But watch yourselves, or you also may be tempted.*"

Notice, Paul said the "spiritual" are the people to "restore," not the religious crowd. Nothing reveals the wickedness of the old nature more than how it treats those who have fallen, not in a military defeat but a moral failure. The religious crowd does not operate on facts and proof but only on whispers, suspicions, and unfounded rumors. Trust me, they would rely on their self-righteous imaginations rather than the truth of God's Word. Their attitude is: "Don't bother me with the facts; my mind is already made up!"

A spiritual man will do all that is necessary to restore a fallen brother or sister. The Greek word for *restore* in Galatians 6:1 is a medical term for "setting a broken bone." Its present tense suggests the necessity of continuing aid and patience in the restoration process.

If you have ever had a broken bone, you know how painful it is. Paul pictures the sinning believer as a broken bone that needs to be set and restored. I love that picture, don't you? A believer who is led by the Spirit will demonstrate love and patience, not shame, guilt, or smug innuendo. A broken bone does not heal overnight. Some broken bones heal faster than others, so the process may be slow. Keep in mind that one size does not fit all in the healing process. Throwing someone on the trash heap because of a moral failure is not what the Word teaches us to do!

2. David Didn't Criticize—He Eulogized

In 2 Samuel 1, we come to one of the most moving eulogies found in the Word of God. David is weeping for Saul and Jonathan and pours his heart out. Pastor Dan Sullivan wrote about David's reaction to Saul's death:

> The next thing he [David] does is out of grief and honor. He writes a song and teaches it to everyone to pay respect and to mourn the death of Saul and Jonathan. He can say more in a song about these guys to immortalize them than

he can in a monument or a speech. His song is a lot like what you'd hear at a funeral. You won't hear about Saul throwing spears or being jealous. You won't hear about him changing around what God wanted to get his own benefits. It's an honor-song. It shows the depth of the relationship David had with the house of Saul, and how deeply he was affected by them.[4]

David took up this lament concerning Saul and his son Jonathan, and he ordered that the people of Judah be taught this lament of the bow (it is written in the Book of Jashar):

A gazelle lies slain on your heights, Israel. How the mighty have fallen!

Tell it not in Gath, proclaim it not in the streets of Ashkelon, lest the daughters of the Philistines be glad, lest the daughters of the uncircumcised rejoice.

Mountains of Gilboa, may you have neither dew nor rain, may no showers fall on your terraced fields. For there the shield of the mighty was despised, the shield of Saul—no longer rubbed with oil.

From the blood of the slain, from the flesh of the mighty, the bow of Jonathan did not turn back, the sword of Saul did not return unsatisfied. Saul and Jonathan—in life they were loved and admired, and in death they were not parted. They were swifter than eagles, they were stronger than lions.

*Daughters of Israel, weep for Saul, who clothed you in scarlet
and finery, who adorned your garments with ornaments of
gold.*

*How the mighty have fallen in battle! Jonathan lies slain
on your heights. I grieve for you, Jonathan my brother; you
were very dear to me. Your love for me was wonderful, more
wonderful than that of women.*

*How the mighty have fallen! The weapons of war have
perished!*

(2 Samuel 1:17-27)

You will notice David does not speak any evil or unkind words
against Saul. It would have been easy to vindicate himself by denigrating
the king, but he chose to do the right thing and honor father and son
who died together on the battlefield.

David praises the "bow of Jonathan" and the "sword of Saul" for their
heroic but unsuccessful fight against the Philistines (see 2 Samuel 1:22).
David describes these two men as war heroes, men worthy of honor and
respect. In the end, they were father and son fighting together, and they
died together as a family!

David began his touching psalm focusing on King Saul. Still, he
ended with the focus on his relationship with Jonathan: *"I grieve for you,
Jonathan my brother; you were very dear to me; Your love for me was wonderful, more wonderful than that of women"* (2 Samuel 1:26). Remember,
David and Jonathan had made a covenant together (see 1 Samuel 18);
it was implemented (see 1 Samuel 19:1-7), and then extended and reaf-
firmed (see 1 Samuel 20-23). Jonathan warned David of his father's plan

to kill him. He protected David, while at the same time he protected his father from his madness.

I can tell you precisely what David was doing. He demonstrated in practical application the principle found in Romans 12:14: *"Bless those who persecute you; bless and do not curse."*

The word for *bless* is a Greek word from which we get the English word *eulogy*, which means to speak well of or to praise. Let me ask you a question. If you have an enemy in your life, could you weep for them? If something terrible happened to them, would you be able to find their good qualities and praise them, much like David did? Look at David—his greatest enemy was dead and he was lying there weeping and grieving.

One would have thought that David would have been dancing on the grave of Saul. His only obstacle to the throne was dead, but instead of celebrating he gave one of the most moving eulogies in the Word of God.

WHAT CAN WE LEARN?

1. David Revealed His Heart

Nothing exposes a person more than when someone falls. David's heart was revealed when he heard the news of Saul's death. No one would disagree that David was guilty of many sins, but in his character he was a man of integrity. He had problems in his life. Every time God spotlighted it, David would turn to the Lord and repent.

How do I know David was a man of integrity? When David's son Solomon became king, God had something to say about David's integrity:

> *As for you, if you walk before me faithfully with integrity of heart and uprightness, as David your father did, and do all I command and observe my decrees and laws, I will establish your royal throne over Israel forever, as I promised David your father when I said, "You shall never fail to have a successor on the throne of Israel."*
>
> (1 Kings 9:4-5)

God is saying to Solomon, "Solomon, if you will walk in integrity like your father, I will establish your royal throne over Israel forever as I promised your father David when I said he will never fail to have a man on the throne of Israel!"

2. Our Integrity Is the Key to a Right Response

What is integrity? Integrity is moral completeness. The word *integrity* means "wholeness" or "completeness." The root word is *integer*, which means "untouched" or "entire."

We are facing a crisis of integrity. It may be the most neglected truth in the Church and business world. There are two forces at work today. The first is the devil, constantly tearing things apart, and the second is

God putting things together! Time is short, and the world is watching us. Let's be honest—if we want to make an impact, our conduct must match our character!

People with integrity are authentic; they do not pretend to be someone they are not. Their lives are like an open book, with nothing to fear. They do not hide behind a mask of religious-sounding words; instead, they say what they mean and mean what they say. Integrity is keeping a commitment when circumstances change and are not what you desire.

3. Jesus Talked about Integrity

Jesus clarified that integrity involves the individual's heart, mind, and will.

Do not store up for yourselves treasures on earth, where moths and vermin destroy, and where thieves break in and steal. But store up for yourselves treasures in heaven, where moths and vermin do not destroy, and where thieves do not break in and steal. For where your treasure is, there your heart will be also.

The eye is the lamp of the body. If your eyes are healthy, your whole body will be full of light. But if your eyes are unhealthy, your whole body will be full of darkness. If then the light within you is darkness, how great is that darkness!

No one can serve two masters. Either you will hate the one and love the other, or you will be devoted to the one and despise the other. You cannot serve both God and money.

(Matthew 6:19-24)

Jesus said the person of integrity will have:

- A single heart: they know they can't love God and the world at the same time (Matthew 6:20-21; 1 John 2:15).

- A single focus: they know that their life must go in the right direction (Matthew 6:22-23; James 1:8).

- A single will: they know they cannot serve two masters (Matthew 6:24; John 8:36).

NOTES

1. https://www.searchquotes.com/search/Death_Of_An_Enemy/ accessed September 19, 2022.

2. This Day in History, "Martin Luther King Jr.'s Home Is Bombed," History.com, https://www.history.com/this-day-in-history/ martin-luther-king-jr-home-bombed-montgomery.

3. Pastor John Lawrence, "How to Respond to the Fall of Our Enemies," November 24, 2010, https://www .calvarychapeljonesboro.org/proverb-a-day/how-to-respond-to -the-fall-of-our-enemies-a-reminder-of-mercy-proverbs-2417-18/ accessed September 19, 2022.

4. Dan Sullivan, "David Finally Sees How He'd React to Saul's Death," July 24, 2017, https://onelifechurch.org/2017/07/david -finally-sees-how-hed-react-to-sauls-death.

11

DAVID AND BATHSHEBA: A CAUTIONARY TALE

It is said that right after great successes comes the greatest risk for a great fall and that is exactly what happened to David.

—Jack Wellman[1]

In the spring, at the time when kings go off to war, David sent Joab out with the king's men and the whole Israelite army. They destroyed the Ammonites and besieged Rabbah. But David remained in Jerusalem. One evening David got up from his bed and walked around on the roof of the palace. From the roof he saw a woman bathing. The woman was very beautiful, and David sent someone to find out about her. The man said, "She is Bathsheba, the daughter of Eliam and the wife of Uriah the Hittite." Then David sent messengers to get her. She came to him, and he slept with her. (Now she was purifying herself from her monthly uncleanness.) Then she went back home. The woman conceived and sent word to David, saying, "I am pregnant."

—2 Samuel 11:1-5

INTRODUCTION

A cautionary tale is a story that gives a warning or makes you understand there is a possible danger or problem. If there were ever a story that fit the definition of a *cautionary tale*, it is the story of David and Bathsheba. The story of David's descent from a king (who could do no wrong) to a man who was willing to throw it all away for a moment of pleasure is truly astounding! David's actions with Bathsheba scream a warning for all of us—danger lies ahead!

The Bible never attempts to cover up the sins of its heroes. The Bible is an honest book that presents the facts about God's people, warts and all, and leaves little to the imagination. But there is one story that captures the imagination like none other—the sordid tale of David and Bathsheba. It has to be the most talked about and written about episode in the entire body of Scripture!

When you think of the life of David, one of two events probably come to your mind. You either remember the time young David slew Goliath; or you remember when David committed adultery with Bathsheba. Both events were monumental moments in the life of David. In the first, David revealed [the] fact of his humility. In the second, David revealed the fact of his humanity. In the first, David proved that he was a man of faith. In the second, David proved that he was a man of flesh. When David met a giant named Goliath, we are privileged to witness his greatest victory. When David met Bathsheba, we are forced to watch his greatest defeat.[2]

I doubt any of us would want to have our sins on display for the whole world to see. If you had asked David, I am sure he would have never guessed that what he did would be made into movies and books. I would not venture to speculate about how many sermons and "life lessons" have been given about David's sin. David found out the hard way that *you may be sure that your sin will find you out* (Numbers 32:23).

David was not only a brilliant composer and gifted musician but also the only person in the Bible God declared "a man after my own heart."

> *After removing Saul, he made David their king. God testified concerning him: "I have found David son of Jesse, a man after my own heart; he will do everything I want him to do."*
>
> (Acts 13:22)

Yet despite his solid heritage, humble beginnings, and a heart devoted to the Lord, David was guilty of adultery, lying, and conspiracy to commit murder. But before you come down too hard on David, remember that none of us are in a position to "cast the first stone." Romans 3:23 says, *"for all have sinned and fall short of the glory of God."* That little word *all* includes you and me!

David was a godly man who did some very ungodly things. His actions betrayed the very God who gave him everything his heart desired. Before you say, "I would never do what David did," I would caution you that we are all subject to the lusts of the flesh when left unguarded by the power of the Holy Spirit. Jeremiah 17:9 declares, *"The heart is deceitful above all things and beyond cure. Who can understand it?"*

An often overlooked statement about David is found in 1 Kings 15:5:

> *For David had done what was right in the eyes of the Lord*
> *and had not failed to keep any of the Lord's commands all*
> *the days of his life—except in the case of Uriah the Hittite.*

God declared that David obeyed all of His commandments and did what was right all the days of his life, but—there is that *except* added at the end of the statement.

Did you catch the phrase at the end? *"except in the case of Uriah the Hittite."* It's terrific for God to brag on you, but He had to throw the exception in there! If we are honest, we all have our exceptions that we don't want to discuss!

————•·◆·•————

DAVID'S DOWNWARD SPIRAL

Let's examine how far this man would go to have his way and what consequences his actions would produce.

Consider David's Sin

David was no ordinary guy hanging out looking for a good time. He was the king—clothed with immense power. David was probably in his early fifties and should have known better than to act like some hormone-fueled teenager!

How does a man like David, a man "after God's own heart," end up in so much self-deception? David had everything his heart desired—wealth, power, and unquestioned loyalty from his subjects. But here we are talking about a man who had everything and was willing to let it all go to feed his lustful desires.

Alan Redpath made an interesting observation about David's downfall:

As I think of what happened (the events are recorded in 2 Samuel 11), of this I am sure, it did not happen all at once. This matter of Bathsheba was simply the climax of something that had been going on in his life for twenty years. For instance, we read: "David took him more concubines and wives (plural, many of them) out of Jerusalem, after he was come from Hebron" (2 Samuel 5:13). This is a direct violation of God's command. In Deuteronomy 17, God laid down specific laws for the one who would be king over his people. There were three things from which he had to abstain: "he shall not multiply horses to himself" (17:16) "neither shall he greatly multiply to himself silver and gold" (17:17) and the third was "neither shall he multiply wives to himself, that his heart turn not away" (17:17).[3]

David obeyed two of three stipulations for the king but failed miserably in the third which was, *"neither shall he multiply wives to himself, that his heart turn not away."* He was not satisfied with the women he had at his disposal, and his passion demanded more and more! As Redpath said, David's sin didn't just happen one day—it was twenty-plus years in the making!

He was presumptuous.

He spent years running, waiting for the day when he would sit on the throne of a united Israel. Now, his vision was realized, and the struggle was over. He lived in the palace enjoying victory over his enemies and untold prosperity. But that was not enough for him. David presumed that because he was king, he could do and have whatever he set his eyes on—that was the first step in his downward spiral. David was too important in his own eyes, and it would cost him dearly.

He was insubordinate.

> *In the spring, at the time when kings go off to war, David sent Joab out with the king's men and the whole Israelite army. They destroyed the Ammonites and besieged Rabbah.* **But David remained in Jerusalem.**
>
> (2 Samuel 11:1)

For some reason, David decided to stay at the palace when he should have been leading his men into battle. We have no idea why David decided it was time to relinquish his role of leading his army to Joab— but he did. We can see the contrast between David's faithful men, willing to sacrifice their lives, and David who stayed at home—out of danger.

Charles R. Swindoll, in his book, *David: A Man of Passion and Destiny*, wrote:

> David was in bed, not in battle. Had he been where he belonged—with his troops—there would never have been

the Bathsheba episode. Our greatest battles don't usually come when we're working hard; they come when we have some leisure, when we've got time on our hands, when we're bored. That's when we make those fateful decisions that come back to haunt us.[4]

He was prideful and self-indulgent.

One evening David got up from his bed and walked around on the roof of the palace. From the roof he saw a woman bathing. The woman was very beautiful, and David sent someone to find out about her. The man said, "She is Bathsheba, the daughter of Eliam and the wife of Uriah the Hittite." Then David sent messengers to get her. She came to him, and he slept with her. (Now she was purifying herself from her monthly uncleanness.) Then she went back home. The woman conceived and sent word to David, saying, "I am pregnant."

(2 Samuel 11:2-5)

If you want to know what "privilege" looks like, watch how David reacts when he sees a beautiful woman. Instead of disciplining himself, he gives in to his desires and becomes careless. He allows his eyes to wander and yields to the "lust of the flesh" and the "lust of the eyes" (1 John 2:16).

James 1:13-15 gives us a New Testament description of just how David's sin unfolded:

When tempted, no one should say, "God is tempting me." For God cannot be tempted by evil, nor does he tempt anyone; but each person is tempted when they are dragged away by their own evil desire and enticed. Then, after desire has conceived, it gives birth to sin; and sin, when it is full-grown, gives birth to death.

- The sight of Bathsheba activated David's desires, and he did not turn away.
- David's desire birthed sin in his mind.
- David gave in to his desire, and this led to his sin.
- David's sin led to death.

It is not a sin to be tempted. David could have avoided this disaster if he had recalled the clear command in Exodus 20:14: *"You shall not commit adultery,"* or the fact that Bathsheba was a man's daughter and a man's wife!

The Bible tells us that Bathsheba was married to one of David's bravest soldiers (see 2 Samuel 23:39). She was also the granddaughter of Ahithophel, who later sided with Absalom in his rebellion against David (2 Samuel 16–17; 23:34).

It takes two to cooperate, but David bears the most significant responsibility. After all, he was the king and could have had more wives if he had wanted them. All he had to do was ask:

I gave your master's house to you, and your master's wives into your arms. I gave you all Israel and Judah. And if all this had been too little, I would have given you even more.

(2 Samuel 12:8)

Instead of telling the Lord he was unhappy with what he had, David decided to take something that didn't belong to him.

David's Cover-Up

The cover-up began as soon as David heard the bone-chilling news: *"The woman conceived and sent word to David, saying, 'I am pregnant.'"* It has been said that the cover-up is always worse than the crime. No one can know for sure, but if he had confessed and repented sooner rather than later, the consequences might have been different. James 1:15 warns us, *"Then, after desire has conceived, it gives birth to sin; and sin, when it is full-grown, gives birth to death."* How fitting are those words in the case of David's sin?

In trying to perpetuate the cover-up, David began a campaign to manipulate the key players in his drama.

First, he tried to manipulate Uriah. Instead of confessing his sin and asking for forgiveness, David did the unthinkable. He sent for Bathsheba's husband and tried to trick him into going home. Had Uriah complied with the king's request to sleep with his wife, David's dilemma would have been solved, or so he thought (see 2 Samuel 11:6-9).

Uriah showed he was the better man when he refused the king's request to go home and be with his wife. It's easy to compare David's self-indulgence and disobedience with Uriah's self-discipline.

David tried one last attempt to trick Uriah by making him drunk. But even a drunk Uriah was a more noble and disciplined man than a sober David (see 2 Samuel 11:11-12)!

Second, he tried to manipulate Joab. David included his army commander in his cover-up. The plan was simple: Uriah had to die. And the best way for him to be removed was to die in battle. It would be a glorious death, and no one would be the wiser. Joab was more than willing to cooperate since this would give him leverage to take advantage of David. It's sad to think, but Uriah carried his death warrant to the battlefield that day (see 2 Samuel 11:14-17).

The plan worked. A brave soldier died that day, and all that was left was for David to put on a show during the week of mourning. No doubt some in the palace probably remarked how thoughtful it was for the king to comfort the widow of Uriah. Little did they know that the king orchestrated the horrible affair, and *soon the widow would be the king's wife* (see 2 Samuel 11:26)!

Third, he tried to manipulate the Lord. David may have fooled others, but a cover-up never works; *"Whoever conceals their sins does not prosper, but the one who confesses and renounces them finds mercy"* (Proverbs 28:13). David thought only three people knew what went on: he himself, Bathsheba, and Joab. But the Lord knew! And that's all that mattered—that *"the thing David had done displeased the Lord"* (2 Samuel 11:27).

David's Cleansing

When a year passed after he committed his sin of adultery and murder, David was sure the cover-up was solid and no one would find out what he had done. He had forgotten that God knows everything and "what he had done displeased the Lord." As the cover-up was unraveling and before he was forgiven, David underwent emotional torment:

When I kept silent, my bones wasted away through my groaning all day long. For day and night your hand was heavy on me; my strength was sapped as in the heat of summer.

(Psalm 32:3-4)

There was no pleasure in David's spirit, but only despair and a desperate desire to be forgiven and restored.

Let me hear joy and gladness; let the bones you have crushed rejoice. Hide your face from my sins and blot out all my iniquity.

Create in me a pure heart, O God, and renew a steadfast spirit within me. Do not cast me from your presence or take your Holy Spirit from me. Restore to me the joy of your salvation and grant me a willing spirit, to sustain me.

Then I will teach transgressors your ways so that sinners will turn back to you.

(Psalm 51:8-13)

David's words of lament in those two psalms reflect what unconfessed sin will do to us spiritually, emotionally, and physically.

- He was weak and physically sick.

- He lost his joy.

- He lost his witness for the Lord.

- He lost his anointing.

- He lost the ability to hear God's voice.

- He lost his spiritual vision.

The Lord revealed David's sin to his pastor, Nathan, the faithful prophet (see 2 Samuel 12:1-7). Nathan did not bring David a blessing but a message of conviction. No doubt it took a lot of courage for Nathan to stand in the presence of the king and declare, *"You are the man!"* (2 Samuel 12:7).

David surrendered to the word of the Lord and admitted his sin. *"Then David said to Nathan, 'I have sinned against the Lord'"* (2 Samuel 12:13). God was ready to forgive David, but in God's government He could not prevent those sins from bringing forth death (see James 1:15). Nathan declared to David, *"Now, therefore, the sword will never depart from your house"* (2 Samuel 12:10).

There would be a fourfold payment for David's sin:

- His secret sin would become public (see 2 Samuel 12:12).

- The baby died (see 2 Samuel 12:15-18).

- His son Absalom killed Amnon, who raped Tamar (see 2 Samuel 13).

- Joab killed Absalom (see 2 Samuel 18:9-17).

Sadly, David would spend the next few years paying for his momentary act of lustful pleasure. The good news is that what started as a sordid affair ended with David back on the battlefield leading his army to victory (see 2 Samuel 12:26-31). David confessed his sins, God forgave him, and with complete confidence he could fight for his nation again.

WHAT CAN WE LEARN?

1. We Can Avoid the Mistakes David Made

Please remember that one of satan's most effective weapons is to accuse us when we fail the Lord (see Revelation 12:7-12). Oh, how the enemy loves to stand before God and point out our sins and shortcomings (see Job 1).

David had plenty of issues, and yes, David committed horrible sins, but God did not condemn him to a life of misery and failure. God did not judge David's entire life based on his sin with Bathsheba. David's sin did not cancel out all the wonderful things he did—not by a long shot! Our God is a redemptive God for kings and for "those less known."

2. Confession and Repentance Is the First Step of Restoration

Once David was willing to confess his sin, God was more than willing to forgive and restore him (see Psalm 37, 51). If God had written David off, you would not have read what God thought about him: *"I have found David son of Jesse, a man after my own heart; he will do everything I want him to do"* (Acts 13:22).

But when we do fall short—it's not over.

- When we fail, God is ready and willing to forgive.
- God is not looking for perfect people—there aren't any!
- Our sin does not cancel out all the good things we have accomplished.
- Satan is a liar; God will use us despite our shortcomings.

3. God's Grace Came Shining Through!

Then David comforted his wife Bathsheba, and he went to her and made love to her. She gave birth to a son, and they named him Solomon. The Lord loved him; and because the Lord loved him, he sent word through Nathan the prophet to name him Jedidiah.

(2 Samuel 12:24-25)

No matter how bad things seem, God can make something good out of our mess. God chose Bathsheba to be the mother of the next king of Israel. *Solomon* means "Peaceable" and *Jedidiah* means "beloved of the

Lord." God turned the curse into a blessing! The Lord restored David to Himself, thereby quelling his inner turmoil and purposing his son as a blessing to all generations.

The overarching lesson of David and Bathsheba should be a warning to all of us to *"be careful that you don't fall"* (1 Corinthians 10:12). We are given the promise God will make a way for us to escape the snare of the evil one (see 1 Corinthians 10:13). We cannot overcome temptation if we allow our sinful desires to overtake us. We must always be on guard and "watch and pray" and never make provision for the flesh: *"Rather, clothe yourselves with the Lord Jesus Christ, and do not think about how to gratify the desires of the flesh"* (Romans 13:14).

NOTES

1. Jack Wellman, "David and Bathsheba Bible Story: Summary, Lessons and Study," The Christian Crier, April 27, 2014, https://www.patheos.com/blogs/christiancrier/2014/04/27/david-and-bathsheba-bible-story-summary-lessons-and-study.

2. Alan Carr, "The Giant That Slew David," https://www.sermonnotebook.org/old%20testament/2%20Samuel%2011_1-27.htm.

3. Redpath, *The Making the Man of God,* 198.

4. Swindoll, *David: A Man of Passion and Destiny,* 302.

12

DAVID'S LEGACY

Even when we read of David now, we know he failed just as much as he succeeded: but it was his sincerity and authenticity that underlined his legacy. It's what separated him from Saul.

—J.S. Park[1]

David son of Jesse was king over all Israel. He ruled over Israel forty years—seven in Hebron and thirty-three in Jerusalem. He died at a good old age, having enjoyed long life, wealth and honor. His son Solomon succeeded him as king.

—1 Chronicles 29:26-28

INTRODUCTION

S tudying the final words of great people of faith is fascinating. I'm referring to men and women who impacted not only the generation they lived in, but influenced many generations after their death.

One such man was William Tyndale. Without his brilliance and courage, the Bible (as we know it) would not have been available to the masses. Tyndale believed the Bible should be accessible to all people, not just the priests. When one of his persecutors questioned this attitude, Tyndale said: "If God spares me, ere many years I will cause a boy that drives the plow to know more of the Scriptures than you do." It is estimated that the Bible is now available in 3,324 languages.

What did Tyndale receive for his devotion to God's Word? On October 6, 1536, at the town of Vilvorde, Belgium, Tyndale was strangled and then burned at the stake for translating the Bible into English. Crying at the stake with a fervent zeal, and a loud voice he spoke his final words: "Lord! open the king of England's eyes."[2]

Many religious people undoubtedly viewed his dedication as a fool's errand. His lasting legacy was his desire to serve God and make the Bible accessible to all people. Tyndale knew his purpose and fulfilled it!

David was also such a man who left a lasting legacy. His reign as king was filled with peaks and valleys, but through it all, his heart was turned toward the Lord. But when the final curtain came down (on his life), he would be remembered for more than just killing a giant. David's heart's desire was leading his nation in peace and righteousness.

- He was shepherd;
- a faithful son;
- a servant;
- a mighty warrior;
- a poet;
- a musician;

- a covenant friend;
- a prophet;
- a priest;
- a king;
- and, most importantly, a man after God's own heart!

One Regret

Through all of David's ups and downs he had one major regret—and it's not what you might suppose.

In 1 Chronicles 28–29 David's final words are a glimpse into his heart and are instructive for us. David reigned over Israel for forty years, and it was now time to share his heart with the people he loved and served:

> *David summoned all the officials of Israel to assemble at Jerusalem: the officers over the tribes, the commanders of the divisions in the service of the king, the commanders of thousands and commanders of hundreds, and the officials in charge of all the property and livestock belonging to the king and his sons, together with the palace officials, the warriors and all the brave fighting men.*
>
> (1 Chronicles 28:1)

The first part of his speech is a reflection on his past. Instead of focusing on his many accomplishments, David shared his *one regret*—a dream that was never fulfilled.

> *King David rose to his feet and said: "Listen to me, my fellow Israelites, my people. I had it in my heart to build a house as a place of rest for the ark of the covenant of the Lord, for the footstool of our God, and I made plans to build it."*
>
> (1 Chronicles 28:2)

David's one desire was to build a temple, and though his motives were pure, the Lord said no!

> *But God said to me, "You are not to build a house for my Name, because you are a warrior and have shed blood."*
>
> (1 Chronicles 28:3)

David did not want to build the temple for selfish gain or personal glory. He desired to honor the Lord by building Him a grand temple that would move the presence of the Lord out of a tent and into a permanent home. That's a worthy cause, wouldn't you agree? But God said no. Reading God's response made me wonder why God would not allow David to complete such a worthy project.

Have you ever thought about why God sometimes says no to people who want to do things to serve and honor Him? *It could be that God has a better perspective than we do.* God can see the whole picture, including the future. Hebrews 4:13 says, *"Nothing in all creation is hidden from*

God's sight. Everything is uncovered and laid bare before the eyes of him to whom we must give an account."

We cannot know all the consequences of our decisions and our actions. As a result, we create a lot of problems for ourselves. If we could see the future, most of our problems would probably be eliminated. So my question is, why doesn't God let us see it? God does not allow us to see the future because He knows we would use it for selfish gain.

We don't have to worry about the future because God's already there. There is no point wasting energy on wondering, worrying, and fretting about tomorrow. After all, what difference does it make when the Father who loves you is already there waiting on you to show up? He's there before you arrive. So if we consult Him over our decisions and are faithful to Him through His Word, we have no worries.

Proverbs 2:7-8 says, *"He holds success in store for the upright, he is a shield to those whose walk is blameless, for he guards the course of the just and protects the way of his faithful ones."* And Proverbs 19:20-21 states, *"Listen to advice and accept discipline, and at the end you will be counted among the wise. Many are the plans in a person's heart, but it is the Lord's purpose that prevails."* He's the one who protects your ways and guards your future!

And it could be that God has a better plan than we do. God said "no" to David not as punishment, but 2 Samuel 7:13 revealed the fact that He had a better plan. He would establish His throne of His kingdom forever. David could never have fully understood the magnitude of God's plan even if God had told it to him. It would be almost one thousand years before the promise would be fully realized. The coming fulfillment of the promise was spoken by Gabriel when he announced the impending birth of the Son of God to Mary. Gabriel declared in Luke 1:32-33:

> *He will be great and will be called the Son of the Most High. The Lord God will **give him the throne of his father David**, and he will reign over Jacob's descendants forever; his kingdom will never end.*

David said, "Lord, You know what I'd like to do? I want to build You a magnificent temple." And God said, "You can't do it. I'm going to raise somebody else who is going to establish My kingdom."

One of the reasons David was a man after God's own heart is in the way he responded when God said no. After finding out he couldn't build the temple, he sat before the Lord. He probably went to the tent where the Ark of the Covenant was located. Listen to David's attitude: *"Then King David went in and sat before the Lord, and he said: 'Who am I, Sovereign Lord, and what is my family, that you have brought me this far?'"* (2 Samuel 7:18).

God was not rejecting David. He just had other plans. David's response reveals how we can have a good attitude when God's answer to our prayers is *no*.

Here's something I have learned the hard way. If you get mad and offended, God will send you right through the same trial again. As one friend said, "You never flunk one of God's tests; you just get to take it over again until you pass!"

WHEN GOD SAYS NO, DO WHAT DAVID DID

First, he responded in submission and not rebellion.

How can we tell that David responded with submission? When you read David's prayer in 2 Samuel 7:18-27, you hear him humbly refer to himself as *"your servant"* at least seven times. David knew he was only a tool in God's hands and had to be a servant. His attitude is the kind that gets God's attention.

We've got to be submissive to God's plan. We cannot look at ourselves as kings, but we've got to look at ourselves as servants. David wasn't God's king. He was God's servant, whom God used to bless the world. So when God says no, we must respond with submission.

Second, he responded with adoration and not self-glorification.

Adoration is simply praising God for who He is. Seven times in that prayer, David says, *Sovereign Lord* (2 Samuel 7:18-27). And the Hebrew word for *Sovereign* is translated as *Lord* in most English Bibles. It signifies that God is the unrivaled ruler and master of creation. And the word translated *Lord* or *God* is *Yahweh,* and it comes from the Hebrew verb *to be.*

How does David express this truth? He said, *"How great you are, Sovereign Lord! There is no one like you, and there is no God but you, as we have heard with our own ears"* (2 Samuel 7:22).

When we live for the Lord, sometimes things do not work out as we think they should. For instance, there may be times when the finances look like they are going bad. Or you have a prodigal child. Whether we like it or not, there are times when God doesn't let things turn out the way we hoped they would. During those times, we sit back and wonder, "Have we done something wrong? Or should we do something different?" We want to know why. When God says no, we must respond with an attitude that allows the fact that God knows best.

Years later, the Lord revealed to David why he could not build His temple. In 1 Chronicles 22:6-10, David shared with his son Solomon why the Lord said no to his desire. There was innocent blood on David's hands.

Then he called for his son Solomon and charged him to build a house for the Lord, the God of Israel. David said to Solomon: "My son, I had it in my heart to build a house for the Name of the Lord my God. But this word of the Lord came to me: 'You have shed much blood and have fought many wars. You are not to build a house for my Name, because you have shed much blood on the earth in my sight. But you will have a son who will be a man of peace and rest, and I will give him rest from all his enemies on every side. His name will be Solomon, and I will grant Israel peace and quiet during his reign. He is the one who will build a house for my Name. He will be my son, and I will be his father. And I will establish the throne of his kingdom over Israel forever.'"

Third, he responded with cooperation.

Many people have their lives all mapped out. But sometimes we pray, study, and prepare, and we have what we think are God's plans, which may or may not materialize. As a result, we feel like because it didn't happen the way we thought it should, it put us on the shelf. Please understand that God doesn't call everybody to build temples. But He does call everybody to be obedient and cooperate with His plan.

One of the greatest examples of David's obedience and cooperation is when God told him that he couldn't build the temple. Instead of putting himself on the shelf, David did everything he could to help people in the future build the temple. He gathered the materials and the craftsmen and contributed much of his own personal fortune (see 1 Chronicles 29:2-5;14-16).

Have you ever thought that when God says no to us perhaps He wants us to help somebody else do what we thought we would get to do in the first place? Not everybody is going to be a missionary, but the local church can help people who are missionaries. Not everybody will be a pastor, but we can do our part to support the church's ministry and the pastor and staff. When God says no, we need to redirect our efforts to help somebody else accomplish the task God has put in our hearts.

While serving God, we must remember the spiritual principle in 1 Corinthians 3:6-7, *"I planted the seed, Apollos watered it, but God has been making it grow. So neither the one who plants nor the one who waters is anything, but only God, who makes things grow."* We cannot all be harvesters. Some of us plant the seed, while others are responsible for watering the seed. That means we all have to trust God for the spiritual harvest.

We need to look to God for the way He wants us to contribute to the final harvest. Whether it is prayer, inviting people to church, the gift of evangelism, teaching a Bible class, or giving financial resources. Everybody has a part and must be willing to give of themselves.

TO SOLOMON, MY SON

David turned his attention toward Solomon and told him what he needed to do to be a man after God's heart.

> *And you, my son Solomon, acknowledge the God of your father, and serve him with wholehearted devotion and with a willing mind, for the Lord searches every heart and understands every desire and every thought. If you seek him, he will be found by you; but if you forsake him, he will reject you forever.*
>
> (1 Chronicles 28:9)

If you want to be a man or a woman after God's heart, follow the pattern of 1 Chronicles 28:9, which says to follow Him and seek Him wholeheartedly. The word *wholeheartedly* means uncut or complete. It refers to an uncut stone. This same concept is found in 1 Kings 6:7, where we read, *"In building the temple, only blocks dressed at the quarry were used, and no hammer, chisel or any other iron tool was heard at the temple site while it was being built."* God said to Solomon, "I don't want the sound of hammers and iron tools heard because they are the sound of war." God wanted his house to be a house of praise and not a place of war.

The uncut stones represent the kind of heart that God wants us to have. Whole, not divided, is what He is after. We must be willing to give it all to Him. We cannot give Him just a piece of our heart. A divided heart can derail you from God's service and God's plan. God does not want our wholehearted service to feed His ego. He wants our whole-hearted service to keep us from sin! Because when your whole heart is given to Him, it can't be distracted by something else.

David also told Solomon to serve God with a *willing mind*. A willing mind means "to delight in or to have pleasure in." So when God wants us to do something, we will find pleasure and delight in doing it. Our attitude as we serve God is as just as important as the service we do.

What Can We Learn?

1. Our Response to God Must Be a Praising Heart

David was one of the most successful men in history. After he killed Goliath, he became a national hero. First Samuel 18:14 says, *"In everything he did he had great success, because the Lord was with him."* Therefore, David had all the possessions, power, and prestige any person could want. How we respond to success will reveal what kind of heart we have.

Success ruins more Christians than failure does. Because when everything is going great, we tend to forget God. When everyone was trying to praise David, he wrote in Psalm 115:1, *"Not to us, Lord, not to us but to your name be the glory, because of your love and faithfulness."* Some of the most significant praise in the Bible is found in the Psalms.

Praise is an exercise in perspective. David clearly kept his wealth and success in perspective. That is why he made a very humbling statement in 1 Chronicles 29:14. He said, *"But who am I, and who are my people, that we should be able to give as generously as this? Everything comes from you, and we have given you only what comes from your hand."*

2. Discover Your Purpose

I can find no better summary of David's life than what the writer of the book of Acts said about him. Acts 13:36 says, *"Now when David had served God's purpose in his own generation, he fell asleep; he was buried with his ancestors and his body decayed."*

David knew his purpose in life and did everything possible to accomplish it without regard for his safety or the opinions of others. Above all else, David desired to please God.

You will notice it says of David that he served God's purpose *in his own generation.* That meant David was only concerned about one thing—his purpose on the earth—nothing more and nothing less. His purpose was to lead his nation in righteousness, peace, and prosperity. I'm not sure if David knew that by serving God in his generation he was also leaving a lasting legacy for many generations to come.

You might say, "But isn't that what kings are supposed to do?" Serving God should be their primary motive, their purpose for living, right? Yes, of course, but that applies to all of us, not just kings.

One of the best insights I have found to the question of purpose was shared by William D. Greenman in his book *Discover Your Purpose, Design Your Destiny, Direct Your Achievement*. He wrote:

> Were you born in this century by chance? Were you born into your family by a fluke of nature? Your country, your race—is it all an accident? If you were a person who never knew your mother or father, or if you were born to parents who were not married, or if you're the offspring of a woman who was raped—does that make you less a creation of God? Can people create human spirits? Can anyone decide when and where and to whom he wants to be born? The answer to all these questions is no. No! You are not an accident or a product of chance. You were ordained of God to be born in your generation, and He knew that if you would give your life to Him, He would be able to use every good and bad part of your life to His glory and to the betterment of those around you. You are totally unique! You were born for a unique purpose![3]

I agree with Greenman. The greatest discovery anyone can make is to know why they were born. Even though David was a man after the heart of God, he was not perfect. Not only are we told about his many accomplishments, but his sins were not covered up either. His life would not be defined by one tragic moment when he defiled himself and defied God.

3. Leave a Legacy Worth Following

David's desire above all else was to leave a lasting legacy that encouraged total devotion to the Lord. Alan Redpath said:

> I love to think about how David got to know God so intimately, as reflected in these words: "Then David gave to Solomon his son the pattern of the porch, and of the houses thereof, and of the treasuries thereof, and of the upper chambers thereof, and of the inner parlours thereof, and of the place of the mercy seat" (I Chron. 28:11).
>
> It may be only a little while until you will pass on the torch to someone else. Can you speak to your dear ones and say to them, "...I can tell you the way to get in: 'knock and it shall be opened unto you'" (Matt. 7:7). Have you preached a Lord Jesus who is completely adequate for an empty life, telling your friends that all the fitness they need to qualify for heaven is to cry to God for mercy? Do you know the pattern of the porch of the temple, and have you made the way clear to another?[4]

David ensured he had something to pass on. A final testimony of this man's life said:

> *David son of Jesse was king over all Israel. He ruled over Israel forty years—seven in Hebron and thirty-three in Jerusalem. He died at a good old age, having enjoyed long life, wealth and honor. His son Solomon succeeded him as king.*
>
> (1 Chronicles 29:26-28)

What more can be said?

What will be said of you?

What will your legacy be for future generations?

David's legacy did not end with his life.

His reign foreshadowed the life and legacy of Christ whose reign will be forever and a day.

You have been born of the warrior clan into the Kingdom of God.

Pay the price, leave a legacy, be a doer of God's word, and live the life you were created for—A WARRIOR'S LIFE!

See you on the battlefield,
Bro. Paul

NOTES

1. J.S. Park, *The Life of King David,* 160.

2. For more details on the life and death of William Tyndale and other martyrs of the faith go to: https://www.biblestudytools .com/history/foxs-book-of-martyrs/the-life-and-story-of-the-true -servant-and-martyr-of-god-william-tyndale.html.

3. William D. Greenman, *Discover Your Purpose, Design Your Destiny, Direct Your Achievement* (Shippensburg, PA: Destiny Image Publishers, 1998), 8-9.

4. Redpath, *The Making the Man of God,* 303-304.

ABOUT PAUL E. TSIKA

P AUL E. TSIKA has been committed to adding value to people's lives for almost 50 years of ministry. He and his wife, Billie Kaye, along with their staff at Restoration Ranch, are dedicated to restoring marriages and rebuilding relationships.

CONTACT PAUL AT:

 Paul E. Tsika Ministries Inc.
46 E Kitty Hawk St
Richmond, TX 77406

(833) 999-9661

www.plowon.org